Danish History Trivia

Journey into the Depths of Denmark's Past with 500 Intriguing Questions and Answers

Welcome Aboard, Check Out This Limited-Time Free Bonus!

Ahoy, reader! Welcome to the Ahoy Publications family, and thanks for snagging a copy of this book! Since you've chosen to join us on this journey, we'd like to offer you something special.

Check out the link below for a FREE e-book filled with delightful facts about American History.

But that's not all - you'll also have access to our exclusive email list with even more free e-books and insider knowledge. Well, what are ye waiting for? Click the link below to join and set sail toward exciting adventures in American History.

Access your bonus here
https://ahoypublications.com/
Or, Scan the QR code!

Table of Contents

INTRODUCTION 1

CHAPTER 1: VIKING VOYAGES 3

CHAPTER 2: DANISH MEDIEVAL MYSTERIES 20

CHAPTER 3: RENAISSANCE ART, SCIENCE, AND ROYAL INTRIGUE 35

CHAPTER 4: KINGS, COURTS, AND CONTROVERSY 51

CHAPTER 5: NAPOLEONIC NEMESES: DANISH DIPLOMACY AND CONFLICT 67

CHAPTER 6: URBANIZATION AND SOCIAL SHIFTS IN DENMARK 84

CHAPTER 7: WORLD WAR WOES: DANISH NEUTRALITY TESTED 101

CHAPTER 8: WW2: DENMARK'S RESISTANCE AND RESILIENCE 116

CHAPTER 9: REBUILDING AND REFORMING DENMARK POST-WAR 129

CHAPTER 10: MODERN DANISH INNOVATION AND CULTURAL EVOLUTION 144

ANSWER KEY 160

CONCLUSION 220

CHECK OUT ANOTHER BOOK IN THE SERIES 223

WELCOME ABOARD, CHECK OUT THIS LIMITED-TIME FREE BONUS! 224

REFERENCES 225

IMAGE REFERENCES 230

Introduction

Denmark, a country with fertile lands and a long history of complex relationships with its neighbors in the Scandinavian region, certainly isn't lacking in interesting facts to uncover. This book will help you do just that while also letting you have tons of fun. It will show you how the Danes went from fierce Vikings to the longest agricultural economy in European history and then to one of the wealthiest countries on the continent.

In between that, you'll learn how Denmark navigated its commitment to neutrality, especially when it was tested or forcefully broken. It is a country, a kingdom, and home to people who rebuilt it many times. So, in a way, learning from their past is like receiving important lessons in finding strength, passion, and success after a (sometimes catastrophic) failure.

One of the most intriguing things you'll discover through this book is that trivia isn't always easy. Some questions will be challenging – but that is why you have the answer keys at the end of the chapter. Still, you should aim to answer the questions to the best of your ability and only then check the answer keys to see if you guessed correctly.

There is no limit on how many times you can read any of the chapters. Anytime you want to look up some interesting tidbit about Demark's history, all you have to do is go to the chapter covering it.

This book isn't just for those who want to measure their knowledge of Danish past times. Even if you do not have experience with history trivia books or have just become interested in learning about history, this book has so much to offer!

You've likely encountered boring history books or ones with only dry facts.

This isn't one of them.

Besides the important events and dates, this book has plenty of little-known information about the people who shaped Denmark's history – you know, the scandalous kings, the unknown heroes and heroines of wars and reforms, and the like.

Here is a little more about what to expect from this book:

- Trivia questions that are easy to understand – but progress from easy to hard questions. This makes it perfect for both beginners and those who already know a little more about Danish history.

- Trivia questions about historical events, famous figures, cultural customs, landmarks, and significant dates.

- "Did You Know?" facts to help expand your knowledge. A little tip: This is where the true fun lies – and these are usually the easiest parts to remember!

- Engaging true or false challenges to test your understanding and quick thinking skills.

By reading this book, you're embarking on a journey of collecting treasure in the form of historical facts. The best part? You can take others on this journey, too. You can use this book for trivia games with friends and family who are also interested in history. They will likely be surprised by some of the facts, just as you will be.

You (and whoever you choose to take with you) can begin this journey whenever you are ready.

Have fun and happy learning!

Chapter 1: Viking Voyages

You have likely heard of Vikings as the mysterious Norse warriors who conquered a major part of Europe. However, did you know that they were also known for their extraordinary sailing and navigational skills? Or were they originally farmers, forced to set on voyages to find a new home after 750 C.E.? Test your knowledge of the history of Danish Vikings in this chapter.

Multiple Choice Questions

1. The Vikings used their ships for:
   A. Warfare
   B. Exploring new lands
   C. Trade
   D. All of the above

2. What type of wood were Viking longships primarily constructed from?
   A. Oak
   B. Cedar
   C. Pine
   D. Larch

3. Which Viking explorer is believed to have reached present-day North America around 1000 AD?

    A. Erik the Red

    B. Ivar the Boneless

    C. Björn Ironside

    D. Leif Ericson

4. What's the name of the technique the Vikings used to build their sturdy vessels?

    A. Click

    B. Clinker

    C. Cross

    D. Catapult

5. What purpose did the carvings on the Viking ships have?

    A. Warding off evil spirits

    B. Identification among tribes

    C. Making the ship look more intimidating

    D. All of the above

6. What types of ships did the Vikings make?

    A. Narrow warships and large cargo vessels

    B. Small cargo ships and large warships

    C. Small vessels for quick travel along the shore

    D. Sturdy ships for transporting people

7. What role did keel construction have in Viking shipbuilding?

    A. Providing stability

    B. Helping with direction

    C. Providing stability and easier direction

    D. Making ships look nicer

8. What did the Vikings trade?

    A. Spices and textiles

    B. Spices, metals, textiles, and slaves

    C. Slaves

    D. Ammunition

9. What made Viking ships good for trade?

    A. Their security, different designs, and ability to navigate harsh conditions

    B. Their speed helped them carry goods faster

    C. Their size

    D. Their frame

10. What advances did Vikings make in their shipbuilding techniques?

    A. Wider hull design

    B. Using smaller sails

    C. A narrower body

    D. Smaller hull design and larger sails

True or False

1. The Vikings used longships for both raiding and trading.

- True
- False

2. The Vikings imported wood for shipbuilding.

- True
- False

3. The vessels were hard to repair.

- True
- False

4. Knarrs had larger hulls.

- True
- False

5. The Vikings used newer designs than previous shipbuilders.

- True
- False

6. The Vikings used a unique oar placement method.

- True
- False

7. They used steering oars instead of rudders mounted on the

starboard.
- True
- False

8. Culture played a big role in Viking shipbuilding.
   - True
   - False

9. The Vikings sailed to North America after the European explorers.
   - True
   - False

10. The first Viking raid in England was in the 10th century.
    - True
    - False

Find the Match

1. Slaves	Female community protectors and additional helpers in raids
2. Jarls	The order of the Viking social structure
3. Family lineage, job title, and wealth	Prisoners of war and people who had fallen into debt
4. Thralls	Rulers and nobility
5. Karls	Trained Viking warriors who fought as if they were in a trance
6. Chiefs and leaders	Craftsmen and free peasants
7. Berserkers	Slaves
8. Vikings	Kings governing the military and important jarls
9. Lesser leaders	People who lead the ceremonies and religious events
10. Shieldmaidens	A term used for those who went on raids

Identify the Picture

1. The picture depicts...

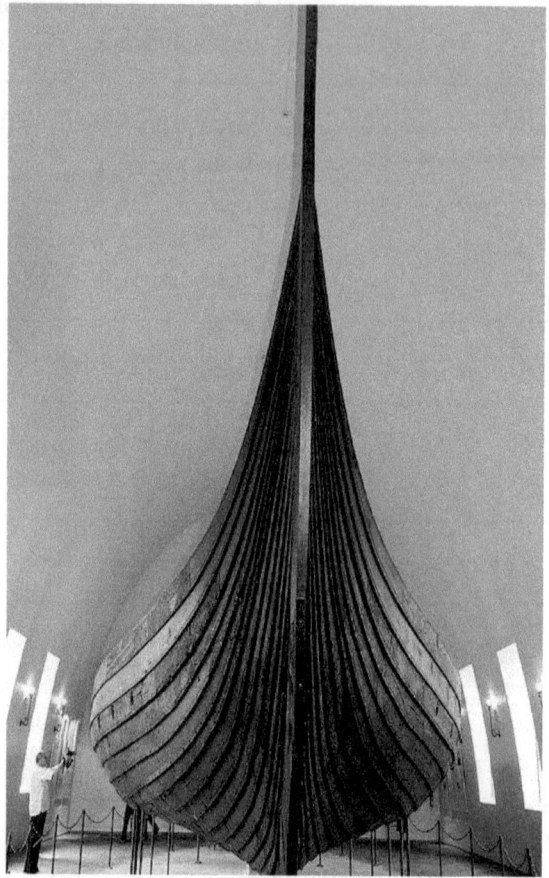

Illustration 1

Response:

_____
_____
_____
_____
_____

2. What structure does the following picture depict?

Illustration 2

Response:

_____
_____
_____
_____
_____

3. What innovation can you see in this picture?

Illustration 3

Response:

_____

_____

_____

_____

_____

3. What made this ship famous?

Illustration 4

Response:

_____
_____
_____
_____
_____

4. This picture shows the Viking's skills because...

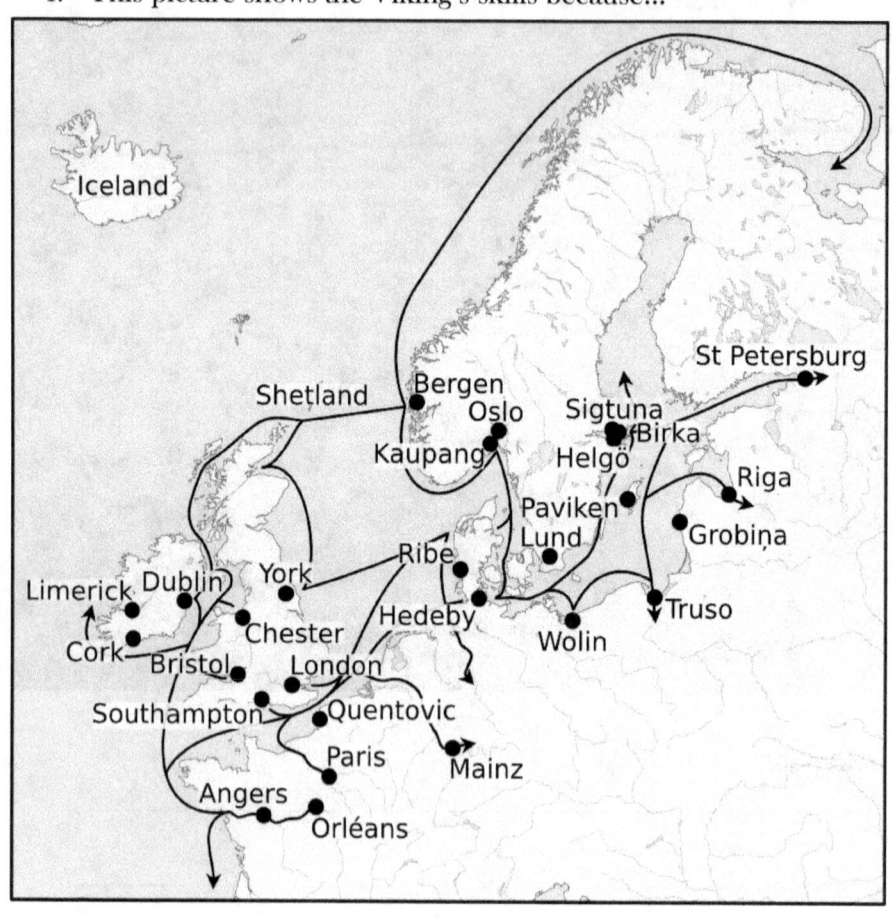

Illustration 5

Response:

_____
_____
_____
_____
_____

5. These objects were found in a Viking burial bound (grave). What do they tell you about Viking society?

Illustration 6

Response:

_____
_____
_____
_____
_____

6. What do you think these objects show about the Vikings' lives?

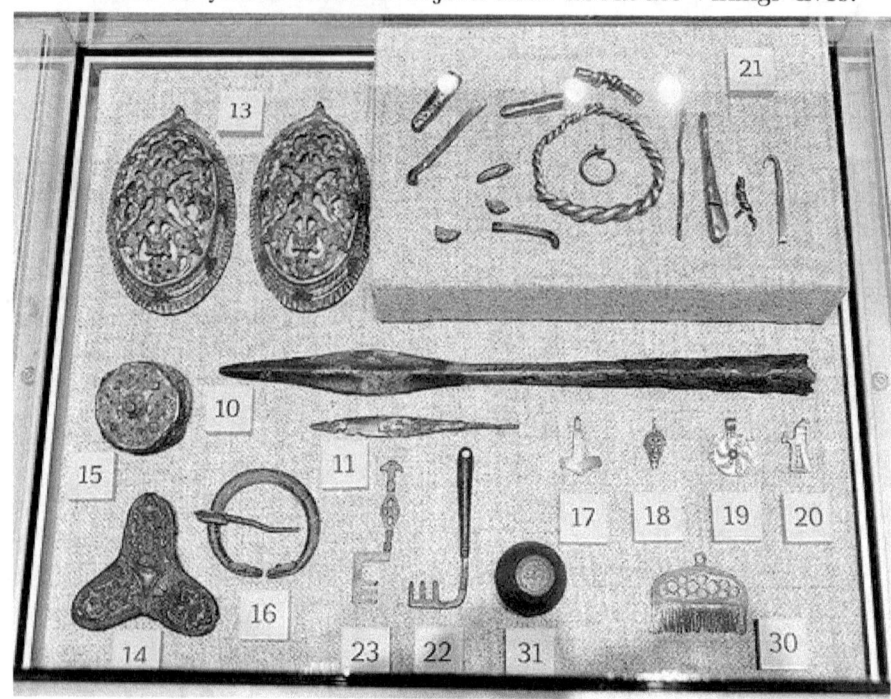

Illustration 7

Response:

_____

_____

_____

_____

_____

7. What do you think this item was used for?

Illustration 8

Response:

_____
_____
_____
_____
_____

8. What was the role of the women in the figure below?

Illustration 9

Response:

_____

_____

_____

_____

_____

9. What was the name of the assembly where Viking leaders gathered to make important decisions?

Illustration 10

Response:

_____
_____
_____
_____
_____

True or False

1. Viking helmets typically had horns protruding from them.
   - True
   - False

2. Vikings were skilled navigators who used the stars and natural landmarks to guide their way.
   - True
   - False

3. The Vikings had fluid gender roles.
   - True
   - False

4. Only those born into important families could become leaders.
   - True
   - False

5. All thralls were people captured in foreign land.
   - True
   - False

6. The first time the Vikings attacked a monastery looking for loot was in 793 A.D. at Lindisfarne.
   - True
   - False

7. The religious leaders believed that the attack at Lindisfarne was a punishment.
   - True
   - False

8. The Vikings began to raid the British shores because they wanted to conquer other nations.
   - True
   - False

9. The English didn't do anything to defend themselves from further attacks.
   - True
   - False
10. The Viking raids had a crucial influence on European history and culture.
    - True
    - False

Chapter 2: Danish Medieval Mysteries

Dark and mysterious, the Middle Ages in Denmark were just as in the rest of Europe. However, the Danes, as always, were a little different. Their unique medieval customs, courtly rituals, and the eventful lives of their famous monarch might surprise you. Go through this chapter and see how much you know about them.

Multiple Choice Questions

1. Which Danish king commissioned the construction of Kronborg Castle, famously known as the setting for Shakespeare's "Hamlet?"
    A. Frederik II
    A. Eric II
    B. Christian IV
    C. Christian V

2. What was the purpose of a medieval tournament?
    A. Entertainment
    B. Show of skills
    C. Exercise
    D. All of the above

3. Which legendary Danish hero is associated with the medieval epic poem "The Heroic Ballads?"

   A. Knud

   B. Valdemar II

   C. Ogier The Dane

   D. Absalon

4. How many times was the Kronborg Castle destroyed?

   A. Once

   B. Twice

   C. Never

   D. Three times

5. What was the role of art in Medieval Denmark?

   A. To show power and status

   B. Communication

   C. Both answers a and b are correct

   D. Trading

6. Who were the Danish Medieval nobility?

   A. Landowners

   B. People from royal families

   C. Military members

   D. Landowners who served in the military and members of important families

7. What settlement structures appeared during the Middle Ages in Denmark?

   A. Towns

   B. A city

   C. Villages

   D. Metropoles

8. Which Danish king was famous for his magnificent buildings?

   A. Christian V

   B. Christian IV

   C. Valdemar II

   D. Eric I

9. Where was Leonora Christina, the daughter of Christian IV, imprisoned?

    A. Kronborg Castle

    B. Frederiksborg Palace

    C. Copenhagen Castle

    D. Rosenborg Palace

10. Were the knight's tournaments dangerous?

    A. Yes, but only for those without experience

    B. Not at all. They were like a game for everyone

    C. There was some danger but not too much

    D. It was a very dangerous activity

Identify the Pictures

1. What does this coin show?

Illustration 11

Response:

_____

_____

_____

_____

_____

2. Name this Danish Medieval tool that is still used today.

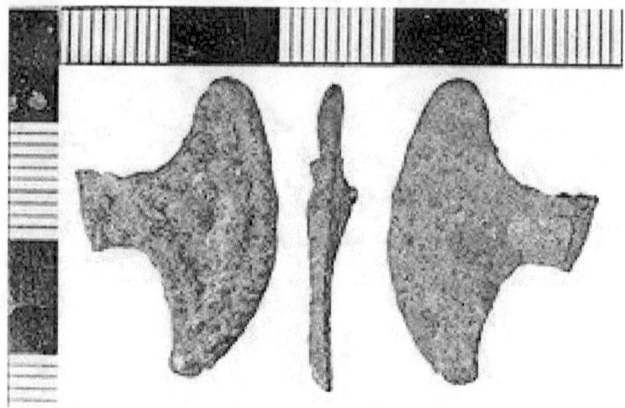

Illustration 12

Response: _____

3. What's in this picture?

Illustration 13

Response:

_____
_____
_____
_____
_____

4. What can you tell about this Medieval coin?

Illustration 14

Response: _____

5. Can you guess what the following items were used for?

Illustration 15

Response:

_____

_____

_____

_____

_____

6. Identify the castle where this picture was taken.

Illustration 16

Response:

_____

_____

_____

_____

_____

7. What do you see in this picture?

Illustration 17

Response:

_____
_____
_____
_____
_____

8. Identify this Danish fortress.

Illustration 18

Response: _____

9. What was this item used for?

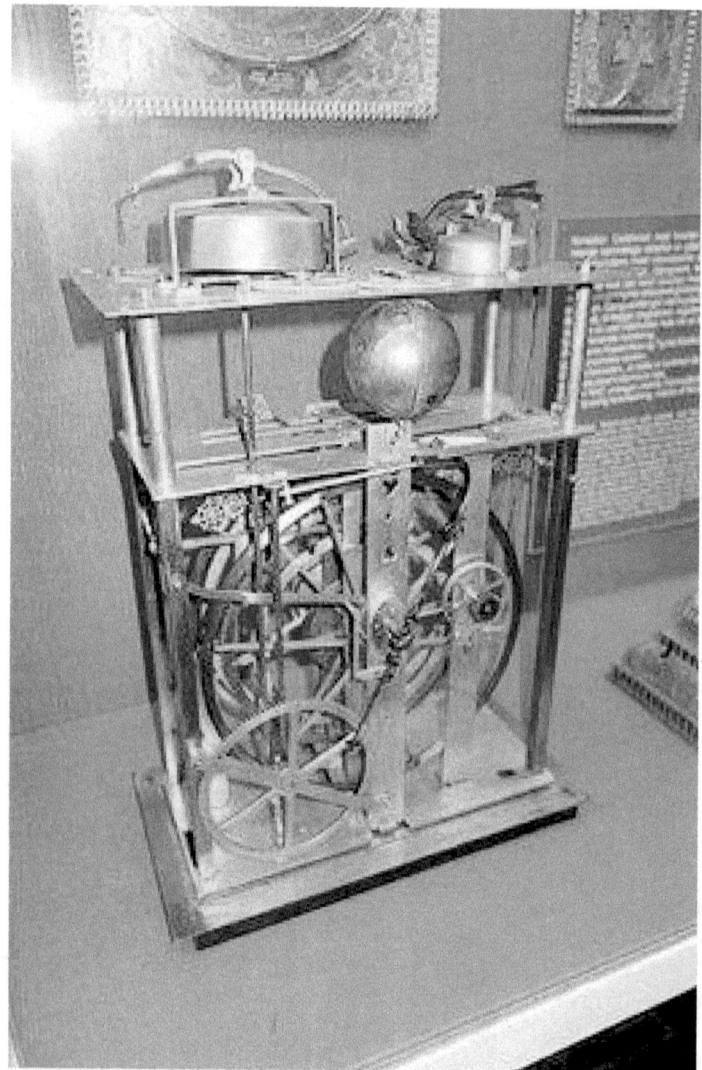

Illustration 19

Response:

_____

_____

_____

_____

_____

10. Who was the Danish royal from the picture married to?

Illustration 20

Response: _____

True or False

1. The medieval period in Denmark spanned from the 5th to the 15th century.

    A. True

    B. False

2. Medieval Danish society was strictly divided into three classes: nobles, clergy, and peasants.

    A. True

    B. False

3. The Kronborg Castle was always used by the royal family of Denmark.

    A. True

    B. False

4. The Dukes of Schleswig were in good relationships with the Danish monarchs.

    A. True

    B. False

5. In 1320, all the royal castles in Jutland were to be demolished.

    A. True

    B. False

6. The Koldinghus Castle was once occupied by the Duke of Holstein.

    A. True

    B. False

7. King Canute IV was the first Danish monarch to be canonized.

    A. True

    B. False

8. Denmark remained a maritime empire until the end of the Medieval period.

    A. True

    B. False

9. The changes in the Danish coin economy allowed the country to regain some of its power.

    A. True

    B. False

10. To save the country from the German princes' attack, the Danish monarch formed an alliance with the kings of Norway.

    A. True

    B. False

Match the Danish Medieval Celebrities to their Actions

1. Holger Danske (Ogier the Dane)	Martyred king of Denmark, sometimes called Knud.
2. Margrethe of Denmark	The national hero whose actions marked the beginning of Denmark's liberation.
3. Canute	Crusader and chancellor to Valdemar the Great.
4. Saxo Grammaticus	One of the few female regents who ruled over several countries in the Middle Ages (Denmark, Norway, and Sweden).
5. Valdemar II	Conquered all the countries from Jerusalem at the center of the world.
6. Absalon	The king who made Denmark prosper through new laws and survived three years in Black Henry's prison.
7. Sir Henrik Svane	Historian who first wrote about Hamlet.
8. Niels Ebbesen	Built one of Denmark's few castles that survived the Medieval times.
9. Esbern the Resolute	Noble knight and lord of Sundkøbing, who held numerous knight tournaments. Fought against many other brave knights not only from Denmark but also from Sweden and other countries.
10. Erik Klipping	Bishop of Roskilde and later Archbishop of Lund.

Multiple Choice Questions

1. What were the manor houses in the Danish Medieval times?

    A. Homes owned by noblemen

    B. Part of the feudal system

    C. Farms in the countryside

    D. All of the above

2. What happened to a manor house or manorial farm if its owner changed its use?

    A. The house or farm lost its manorial status

    B. The house or farm remained a manor

    C. Another manor was built beside it

    D. The owner had to choose another house or farm as a manor

3. What is a commonly used name for the Danish Empire from the Medieval times (12th and 14th century)?

    A. The Great North Sea Empire

    B. Valdemarian Kingdom

    C. Kalmar Union

    D. Kingdom of Denmark

4. What countries made the Kalmar Union?

    A. Denmark and Norway

    B. Denmark and Sweden

    C. Denmark and England

    D. Norway, Sweden, and Denmark

5. Was courtly culture (the behavior at the courts) different in Denmark than in the rest of Scandinavia?

    A. Yes, it was different, but only from Norway

    B. It was only different from Sweden

    C. It was the same as it was in Norway and Sweden

    D. It was different than it was in Sweden and Norway

6. What made the Danish court different from the others?

    A. Different traditions

    B. Language

C. Customs of nobility

D. The king's behavior

7. **How did Margrethe, the daughter of the Danish king, Valdemar IV, keep Denmark from ruin?**

A. By ruling instead of others

B. By convincing her husband to unite their countries

C. By being a strong female regent

D. All of the above

8. **Which two brothers had the most shocking conflict in Medieval Denmark?**

A. Cnut VI and Valdemar II

B. Erik IV and Abel

C. Harthacnut and Cnut II

D. King Erik III and Niels

9. **How did the Danes choose their king in the Middle Ages?**

A. The kingship automatically went from father to the firstborn son

B. The kingship went to any family member who was old enough to rule

C. The king was elected by voting at the thing

D. The king was elected by the nobles at the court

10. **Who were the Hvide?**

A. A powerful magnate kin group

B. Pirates

C. The Danes' enemies

D. A group of peasants

Chapter 3: Renaissance Art, Science, and Royal Intrigue

When you hear the phrase *Renaissance*, you probably think of colorful paintings with religious motives. The cultural rebirth of classicism in Denmark had seen plenty of this and much more. For example, did you know that one of the biggest scientific discoveries was made by Danish Renaissance astronomers? In this chapter, which is packed with trivia questions about the Danish Renaissance, you can learn about this and many other facts about events and people who left a lasting legacy.

Multiple Choice Questions

1. Which Danish astronomer is known for his groundbreaking observations of the heavens, including the discovery of new stars and comets?

    A. Tycho Brahe

    B. Sophia Brahe

    C. Ole Rømer

    D. Christen Sørensen Longomontanus

2. What influential work did the Danish philosopher Tycho Brahe publish in 1596 detailing his astronomical observations?

    A. A detailed description of planetary positions

    B. Epistolarvm astronomicarvm libri (containing his theories about the structure of the Solar system)

C. A detailed description of the Solar system

D. A new Solar system model

3. Which astronomer contacted Tycho Brahe at the end of the 16th century, asking him for the details of his research?

    A. William of Hesse

    B. Christen Sørensen Longomontanus

    C. Johannes Kepler

    D. Rene' Descartes

4. Which issue did Tycho Brahe suggest Kepler solve?

    A. The orbit of the planets

    B. The orbit of the Sun

    C. The relationship between the Sun and Mars

    D. The unusual movement of Mars

5. How did King Frederik II prevent Tycho Brahe from leaving Denmark?

    A. By offering him money

    B. By telling him he will be punished if he tried to leave

    C. By granting him his own island and observatory

    D. By asking him to be the king's consultant

6. Besides Frederik II and Johannes Kepler, which other prominent person supported Tycho Brahe's work?

    A. Holy Roman Emperor Rudolf II

    B. Niels Steensen

    C. Rasmus Bartholin

    D. Christian V

7. Who was the Danish king known as the "Father of the Danish Renaissance" for his support of the arts and sciences?

    A. Frederik II

    B. Christian IV

    C. Christian V

    D. Frederik I

8. Why did Frederik II begin to support science?

   A. He was interested in science but was too busy to dedicate his time to it himself

   B. He thought it would make him a stronger leader

   C. He used science to strengthen his kingdom

   D. He didn't want to stay behind other European leaders who also supported science

9. How did Christian IV want to preserve Denmark's history?

   A. By paying writers to write books about Danish history

   B. Paying to build a building that would show the elements of history

   C. By founding several cities

   D. All of the above

10. How did Christian IV want to show Denmark in the history books?

   A. As a kingdom stronger than any of its neighbors

   B. As a kingdom with great traditions

   C. As a modern kingdom

   D. As a peaceful kingdom

True or False

1. The word *renaissance* means return.

   - True
   - False

2. The Reformation occurred during the Renaissance Period.

   - True
   - False

3. During the Renaissance, the king was the supreme protector.

   - True
   - False

4. The Danish language has become more popular.

   - True
   - False

5. The royal court was unhappy with the arrival of the Renaissance.
   - True
   - False

6. The kings were the only ones who displayed magnificent and costly lifestyles.
   - True
   - False

7. The lavish lifestyles of some lead to significant contrasts within society.
   - True
   - False

8. The Danish kings successfully made Denmark into a dominant power in the Baltic area.
   - True
   - False

9. The Castle of Kronborg at Elsinore was built in 1590.
   - True
   - False

10. The Danish Renaissance is still one of the most preserved periods in the country's history.
    - True
    - False

Match the Answers

1. Christiern Pedersen	Author of the play, The Miserly Rascal.
2. Anders Sørensen Vedel	Writer of Danish Baroque poetry and founder of the first Danish newspaper, Den danske Mercurius.
3. Pedar Palladius	A true poetry master who wrote in every poetry genre that was popular during the Renaissance.
4. Hieronymus Justesen Ranch	Writer of Hexaëmeron and translator of the Psalms.
5. Anders Bording	A talented spokesperson and supporter of the Danish Lutheran Church.
6. Thomas Kingo	One of the most famous historians of the Danish Renaissance.
7. Anders Arrebo	Author of Monumenta Danica, a book on runic inscription. He was a scholar rather than an artist.
8. Ole Worm	Author of the Visitation Book.
9. Arild Huitfeldt	Humanist and writer who translated Martin Luther's publications and the New Testament.
10. Hans Tausen	Historian who translated Saxo Grammaticus Gesta Danorum into Danish and published the first collection of Danish medieval ballads.

True or False

1. The Renaissance period in Denmark saw a revival of interest in classical Greco-Roman literature and philosophy.
   - True
   - False

2. Renaissance artists in Denmark primarily focused on religious themes in their artwork.
   - True
   - False

3. Some of the art was directed for or against the Roman Catholic Church.
   - True
   - False

4. The Bible was translated into Danish before the Renaissance.
   - True
   - False

5. Human personality and individuality were very important to Renaissance artists.
   - True
   - False

6. Most of the most outstanding architectural achievements from the Renaissance era were seen in cathedrals and other religious buildings.
   - True
   - False

7. Jorgen Friborg was a master architect who rebuilt Frederiksborg Castle.
   - True
   - False

8. In sculpture and painting, the French Baroque style was dominant.
   - True
   - False

9. The Bartholin family made a significant contribution to science.

- True
- False

10. The first two faculty appointments in the philosophical sciences date from the Renaissance period.

- True
- False

Identify the Pictures

1. What is shown in the picture?

Illustration 21

Response: _____

2. What's unusual about the statue's face?

Illustration 22

Response:

_____
_____
_____
_____
_____

3. Can you identify the person in this picture?

Illustration 23

Response: _____

4. Can you identify the painter's influence in this picture?

Illustration 24

Response:

_____

_____

_____

_____

_____

5. What does this picture show?

Illustration 25

Response:

_____

_____

_____

_____

_____

6. Can you identify the building in this picture?

Illustration 26

Response: _____

7. What does this picture depict?

Illustration 27

Response:

_____

_____

_____

_____

_____

8. Identify this picture.

Illustration 28

Response:

_____
_____
_____
_____
_____

9. Identify this picture.

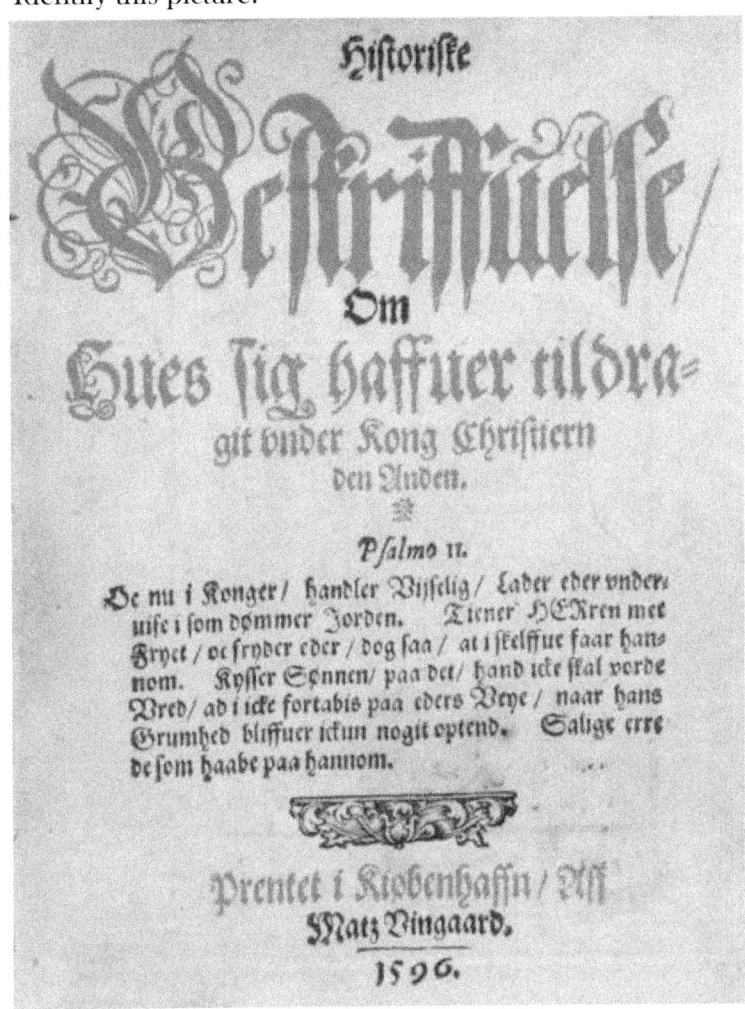

Illustration 29

Response:

_____

_____

_____

_____

_____

10. Who is in this picture?

Illustration 30

Response: _____

Chapter 4: Kings, Courts, and Controversy

This chapter offers questions about the period of Danish absolute monarchy – which was absolutely grand in every sense. From the king's power to how the monarchs and their favorite advisors wanted to show their strengths to the controversies, everything was complex and a little bit exaggerated. Yet, the person had an undeniable influence on Denmark's history, and you'll soon see why.

Multiple Choice Questions

1. Which Danish king is known as the heir of the "Sun King of the North" for his lavish court and absolute rule?
    A. Christian V
    B. Christian IV
    C. Frederik II
    D. Frederik III

2. What influential document, issued by King Christian V, strengthened royal authority in Denmark?
    A. Danish Law
    B. Monarchy Rules
    C. Absolutism Guide
    D. Royal Laws

3. What was the consequence of having a centralized and absolute rule?

   A. The manorial lords became more powerful

   B. The manorial lords lost their influence

   C. The king's power became weaker

   D. The manorial lords became the king's advisors

4. What was the dominant political ideology for the monarchy from the mid-18th century?

   A. Reformation

   B. Absolute reformation

   C. Enlightened absolutism

   D. Partial enlightenment

5. Who was the powerful advisor to King Christian VII, often considered the de facto ruler of Denmark during the late 18th century?

   A. Peder Schumacher Griffenfeld

   B. Johann Friedrich Struensee

   C. Paul-Henri Mallet

   D. Johann Hartwig Ernst von Bernstorff

6. Which ruler started the Scanian War against Sweden in 1665?

   A. Christian VII

   B. Christian V

   C. Frederik IV

   D. Frederik III

7. The main central institutions during the absolute monarchy were

   A. The Danish chancellery and the treasury

   B. The treasury and the war chancellery

   C. The German chancellery

   D. The Danish chancellery, the German chancellery, the treasury, and the war chancellery

8. When was the Danish Code introduced?
    A. 1683
    B. 1687
    C. 1783
    D. 1787
9. The absolute monarchy also resulted in...
    A. Elective monarchy
    B. Manorial monarchy
    C. Hereditary monarchy
    D. None of the above
10. Why was the law of precedence, issued by Christian V in 1671, significant?
    A. Gave exclusive rights to offices of state
    B. Gave access to land ownership to more people
    C. Left nobility without estate privileges and status
    D. Established social hierarchy based on royal service instead of birth

True or False

1. The Danish monarchs of the absolute monarchy period wielded unchecked power without any limits or constraints.
    • True
    • False
2. The absolute monarchy granted more power to Denmark from its beginning to its end.
    • True
    • False
3. By 1849, Denmark had become a small and poor country.
    • True
    • False
4. More people moved to larger towns and the capital during the absolute monarchy.
    • True
    • False

5. Absolutism made the hierarchies in the society of estates clearer.
   - True
   - False

6. The king's personality often determined the social character of the royal court.
   - True
   - False

7. Public opinion became extremely powerful during the absolute monarchy.
   - True
   - False

8. The absolutist kings had noble servants to help them with the administration of court matters.
   - True
   - False

9. Religion continued to influence absolutism until the mid-19th century.
   - True
   - False

10. Absolute monarchy in Denmark ended with the adoption of the Danish Constitution in 1849.
    - True
    - False

Match the Answers

1. Christian VI	The first absolute monarch who tried to limit the civil servant's power.
2. Frederik V	Crown Prince Frederik's teacher and a temporary ruler.
3. Lord Chamberlain A.G. Moltke	The estate owner and leader of the Financial Chamber resolved the issue of unpaid labor (which Struensee caused).
4. Frederik III	Joined forces with Napoleon, which led to a devastating attack from the British army.
5. Christian V	The most scandalous ruler, known for liking to party a little too much.
6. Ove Høegh-Guldberg	The most religiously influenced absolutist monarch.
7. Caroline Mathilde	One of Frederik's closest advisors.
8. Karl Peter Ulrich	Adopted the "divide and rule" policy, which meant civil servants had no specific power.
9. Crown Prince Frederik VI	A Gottorp duke, who allowed the Danish king to take over Schleswig and Holstein.
10. Christian D.F. Reventlow	Queen to Christian VII had a close relationship with Johann F. Struensee.

Multiple Choice Questions

1. What were the duties of counts and barons during the absolute monarchy?

    A. Reporting to the royal court

    B. Collecting taxes

    C. Collecting fines and reporting crimes to the manorial court

    D. Ruling over the poor

2. How much influence did civil servants have over state matters?

    A. They didn't have much influence

    B. They were very powerful

    C. They only had power in some matters

    D. Only some of them had a little more power than before

3. How did Frederik III personalize the court letters and documents?

    A. By putting his signature on everything

    B. By putting the number III on everything

    C. By putting F3 on everything

    D. He didn't personalize anything

4. How did Christian V cause controversy among the court officials?

    A. By giving out harsh punishments

    B. By naming favorites and making court officials compete

    C. By not recognizing their hard work

    D. By being unfair when rewarding them

5. Who ended the rule of Johann F. Struensee?

    A. Frederik V

    B. Christian VII

    C. The Crown Prince Frederik

    D. Juliane Marie

6. Why did the place of the king's residence change during the absolute monarchy?

    A. It was previously damaged

    B. It needed a new look

C. It was too small

D. The queen asked the king to change it

7. Which absolute monarch built a new district in Copenhagen?

A. Frederik V

B. Frederik IV

C. Christian V

D. Christian VII

8. How did court members spend their time?

A. By playing cards and chess

B. By going to balls and parties

C. By attending royal dinners

D. All of the above

9. When did club culture develop in Copenhagen?

A. 1680

B. 1750

C. 1780

D. 1720

10. When was the Supreme Court established?

A. 1771

B. 1661

C. 1671

D. 1761

Identify the Pictures

1. Whose "signature" is this?

Illustration 31

Response: _____

2. What is in this picture?

Illustration 32

Response:

_____
_____
_____
_____
_____

3. Who is on this medal?

Illustration 33

Response:_____

4. Who is the author of the following portrait?

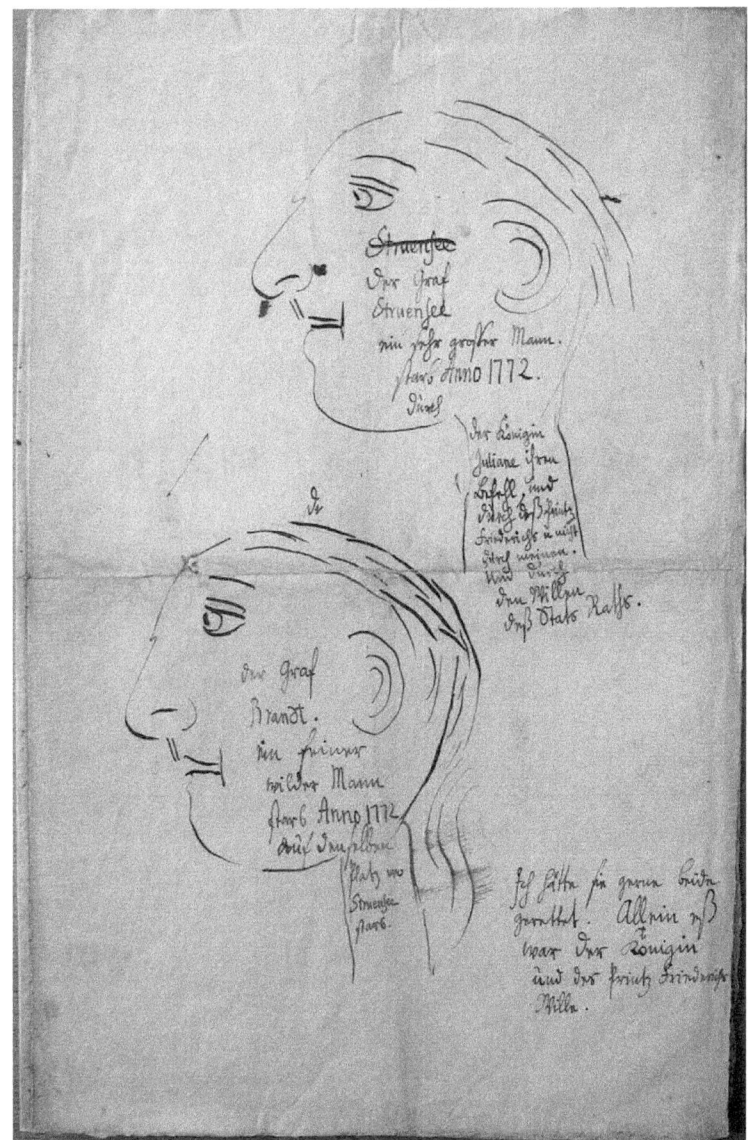

Illustration 34

Response: _____

5. What does this picture depict?

Illustration 35

Response:

_____
_____
_____
_____
_____

6. Who is shown in this portrait?

Illustration 36

Response: _____

7. What type of building is in this picture?

Illustration 37

Response: _____

8. What is in this picture?

Illustration 38

Response: _____

9. What significant event is pictured here?

Illustration 39

Response:

_____
_____
_____
_____
_____
_____

10. What do you think the purpose of this ship was?

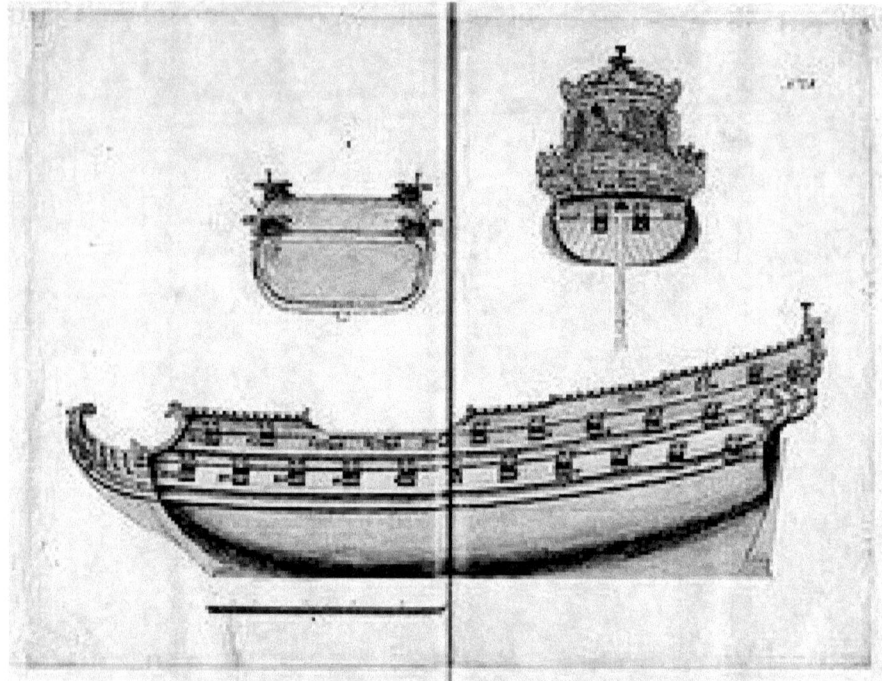

Illustration 40

Response:

_____

_____

_____

_____

_____

Chapter 5: Napoleonic Nemeses: Danish Diplomacy and Conflict

The Napoleonic era was challenging for all countries on the European continent, and Denmark was no exception. Denmark-Norway wanted to remain neutral in the conflict brewing between Britain and France but wasn't able to. This chapter brings you many interesting questions and facts about this trying period – during which Denmark also had to fight with its arch-enemy, Sweden!

True or False

1. Denmark-Norway remained neutral during the early years of the Napoleonic Wars.
   - True
   - False

2. The Treaty of Kiel in 1814 resulted in Denmark ceding Norway to Sweden.
   - True
   - False

3. France and Russia put pressure on Denmark to join its fleet to Napoleon's.
   - True
   - False

4. Britain feared that the Danish naval feet would defeat the British if Denmark joined Napoleon.
   - True
   - False

5. Denmark wanted to sign a treaty with Great Britain.
   - True
   - False

6. The British forces began their attack by surrounding Zealand.
   - True
   - False

7. Denmark surrendered its Nordic ports to the British willingly.
   - True
   - False

8. Denmark expected Napoleon to attack from the direction of the Schleswig-Holstein area.
   - True
   - False

9. Denmark remained allied with Great Britain throughout the Napoleonic wars.
   - True
   - False

10. Frederik VI faced criticism after the disastrous end of the war.
    - True
    - False

Match the Answers

1. Edmund Bourke	A naval officer and Privy Counselor who played a crucial role during Denmark's state of armed neutrality.
2. Christian Bernstorff	The commander who defended Copenhagen from the British forces in 1801.
3. Niels Rosenkrantz	Danish naval officer who organized the Norwegian defenses against Sweden and then Britain.
4. Steen Andersen Bille	A Danish naval officer known for his heroic actions and sacrifice at the Battle of Zealand Point.
5. Hinrich Ernst Peymann	Danish-Norwegian Naval commander who led several battles against the British navy on the waters of the Danish West Indies.
6. Johan Olfert Fischer	Danish nobleman who was also the governor of Norway during the Napoleonic wars. Later became the governor of Schleswig and Holstein.
7. Lorentz Fisker	The foreign minister who worked closely with the then Prince Regent Frederik VI until 1810.
8. Peter Willemoes	The Danish negotiator who signed the peace treaty in Kiel.
9. Carl Wilhelm Jessen	The commander of Danish forces during the Second Battle of Copenhagen in 1807. Also signed the capitulation at Hellerupgård.
10. Prince Frederik of Hesse	He was the second foreign minister under Frederik VI's rule and the one who participated in the Napoleonic wars alongside his king.

Multiple Choice Questions

1. What was the name of the naval battle in 1801 where the Danish fleet famously resisted British attacks during the Napoleonic Wars?

    A. Baltic Battle

    B. Danish Battle

    C. First Battle of Copenhagen

    D. Northern Battle

2. Which Danish prince served as a field marshal in the French army under Napoleon Bonaparte?

    A. Charles III John

    B. Christian Frederik

    C. Crown Prince Frederik

    D. Prince Christian August

3. What was the consequence for Denmark of joining Napoleon's Continental System, which aimed to blockade British trade?

    A. Severing alliances with Russia

    B. Further aggravating the relations with Sweden

    C. Ending up on the losing side of the war

    D. All of the above

4. How did the Danish Prince Regent react to Napoleon's advance to the border of Holstein?

    A. By signing a new naval plan

    B. By withdrawing his army from the southern districts of Holstein

    C. By bringing more forces to the southern districts of Holstein

    D. None of the above

5. Why was Frederik VI so confident in Napoleon's success?

    A. He saw Napoleon's advance in Europe, although no one could defeat the French emperor.

    B. He was a great admirer of Napoleon's strong character

    C. He believed that the Russians were outnumbered and weaker

    D. He thought that Napoleon's tactic was flawless

6. **What was Frederik V's condition for breaking his alliance with Napoleon?**

    A. Guaranteed immunity

    B. Financial compensation

    C. More support for Norway

    D. Guaranteed territorial integrity of his state

7. **What were the conditions of the Treaty of Fontainebleau?**

    A. Mutual support, Denmark joining the Continental system, and France compensating Denmark's losses during the war.

    B. Denmark joining the Continental system without any compensation

    C. Neither party could negotiate peace without the other

    D. Denmark guaranteeing the integrity of France

8. **What did Great Britain want to accomplish by taking over the Danish ports?**

    A. Continuing trade to supply the country with produce

    B. Continuing trade to supply the allies with metals and grain

    C. Gaining access to more export/import opportunities

    D. Gaining access to strategic defense/offense points

9. **Did the Danes eventually understand that the French would not pay for their losses?**

    A. No, they never thought they wouldn't be compensated

    B. They suspected but weren't sure

    C. They knew, but they focused on preserving their state's integrity

    D. No, they didn't know, even though they were warned by the British

10. **What treaty did Frederik VI propose to Napoleon in 1812?**

    A. A treaty for support against Russia in exchange for Holstein

    B. A treaty for support against Sweden in exchange for financial support

    C. A treaty for support against Britain and Sweden in exchange for Norway's support

D. A treaty for support against Russia in exchange for a commercial treaty

True or False

1. The Napoleonic wars had a powerful effect on Denmark's economy from the beginning.
   - True
   - False

2. Denmark's decision to side with Napoleon was only for economic and defensive reasons.
   - True
   - False

3. Denmark was forced to declare bankruptcy after the wars.
   - True
   - False

4. Denmark-Norway was also concerned about defending themselves from a potential Swedish attack.
   - True
   - False

5. Initially, Denmark kept most of its defense forces near Copenhagen.
   - True
   - False

6. A conflict with Napoleon would have led to catastrophic consequences for the twin kingdom.
   - True
   - False

7. Denmark wanted to seek mediation before 1814.
   - True
   - False

8. Napoleon supported his Danish ally against the Swedish aggression.
   - True
   - False

9. Denmark didn't want to help the Norwegians become independent.
    - True
    - False

10. Napoleon's defeat wasn't a surprise to Denmark.
    - True
    - False

Identify the Pictures

1. Which battle is shown in this picture?

Illustration 41

Response:

_____

_____

_____

_____

_____

2. Which country had this Royal of Arms until the early 19th century?

Illustration 42

Response:

_____

_____

_____

_____

_____

3. What is depicted in this picture?

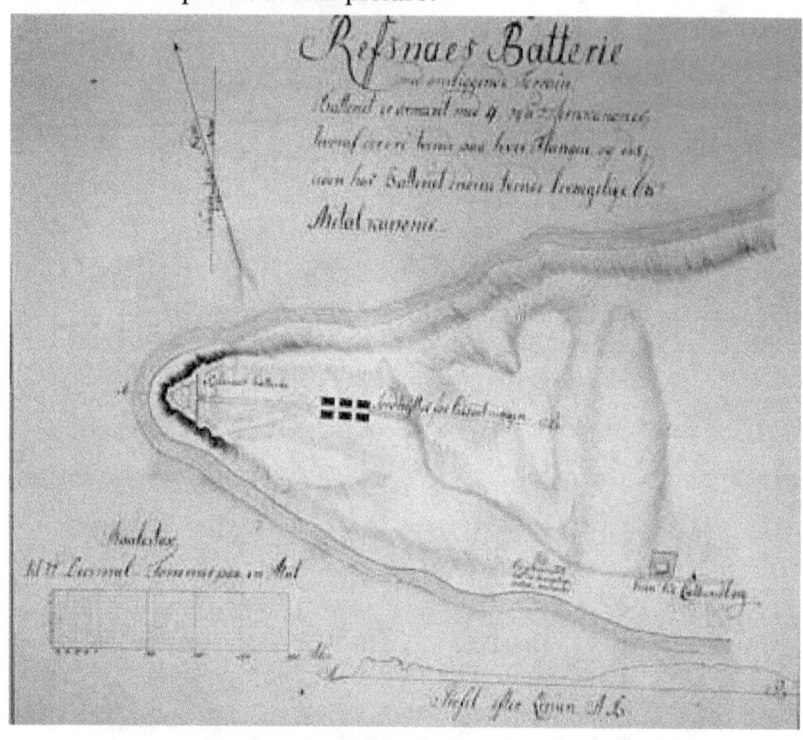

Illustration 43

Response:

_____

_____

_____

_____

_____

4. Can you identify the territory shown on the map?

Illustration 44

Response:

_____
_____
_____
_____
_____

5. The only man in Denmark who predicted that Napoleon would lose. Who was he?

Illustration 45

Response:

_____

_____

_____

_____

_____

6. Identify the ship in the picture.

Illustration 46

Response:

_____

_____

_____

_____

_____

7. Which battle is shown in this picture?

Illustration 47

Response:

_____

_____

_____

_____

_____

8. He was the brave tactician who, unfortunately for the Danes, helped defeat Napoleon. Who was he?

BENNINGSEN

Illustration 48

Response:

9. Which Napoleonic era event is pictured here?

Illustration 49

Response:

_____

_____

_____

_____

_____

10. Denmark also participated in other battles during the Napoleonic Wars. Which one is shown in the picture?

Illustration 50

Response:

_____

_____

_____

_____

_____

Chapter 6: Urbanization and Social Shifts in Denmark

Ever since the first Viking settlements, Denmark has been a proud agricultural country. Unfortunately, after losing major chunks of its territory and getting into serious debt at the beginning of the 19th century, Denmark lost fundamental income resources. To add to the country's problems, the population began to grow very quickly, which meant more people to feed, employ, and pay. This chapter shows how Denmark took advantage of the Industrial Revolution to turn its economy around, reviving or building new thriving industries. You'll also learn about the issues of urbanization (people moving to the cities) and social shifts created during the period.

Multiple Choice Questions

1. What led to Denmark's urbanization during the Industrial Revolution?

    A. Population growth

    B. Lack of work in the countryside

    C. Higher ability to sell craft products in the cities

    D. All of the above

2. When did the first multinational companies appear in Denmark?

    A. After 1850

    B. After 1900

C. After 1880

D. After 1910

3. What did the end of the traditional structure of the Danish economy mean for the country and its citizens?

    A. The country was no longer able to live on agriculture alone

    B. The country had to focus even more on agriculture

    C. The country had to focus on strengthening its economy

    D. The farmers had to abandon agriculture altogether and work in the cities

4. What type of economy did Denmark embrace during the Industrial Revolution?

    A. Planned

    B. Market-oriented

    C. Command

    D. Mixed

5. What other factors made urbanization possible besides job opportunities in the cities and larger towns?

    A. Growth of transport infrastructure

    B. New telecommunication systems

    C. New business strategies

    D. Something else

6. Which two classes were the urban societies divided into?

    A. Business and working

    B. Working and trade

    C. Trade and middle

    D. Middle and working

7. What was the main value middle-class Danes lived by?

    A. Earning and managing their own money

    B. Earning more money than the poorer working class

    C. Earning enough money to spend how they wanted

    D. Living a simple life

8. What was the major difference between urban middle-class and working-class societies?

    A. Where they lived

    B. How they spent their days

    C. How much money they earned

    D. How much education they had

9. What was one major problem with urbanization in Copenhagen and other larger Danish cities?

    A. Lack of work

    B. Lack of hygiene

    C. Lack of space

    D. Lack of poor relief

10. How did craft businesses develop in the urban areas?

    A. They struggled due to the lack of demand

    B. They grew very slowly

    C. They grew fast

    D. Some industries developed while others disappeared

Match the Answers

1. Businessmen	Unskilled (low-paid) workers.
2. Service trade workers	Working class women.
3. Civil Servants	Major landowners in urbanized towns.
4. Police	Upper middle class.
5. Housewives	Upper middle class.
6. Bricklayers	Lower middle class.
7. Housemaids	Skilled (higher paid) workers.
8. Teachers	Social elite.
9. Aristocratic landowners	Public servants/Lower middle class.
10. Doctors	Upper middle class/Lower middle class.

Identify the Pictures

1. What do you think the purpose of this building was?

Illustration 51

Response:

_____

_____

_____

_____

_____

2. What does this picture show you?

Illustration 52

Response:

_____

_____

_____

_____

_____

3. Even in the cities on or near the mainland, gardening was often a woman's job. Why?

Illustration 53

Response:

_____

_____

_____

_____

_____

4. What effect of the Industrial Revolution can you see in this picture?

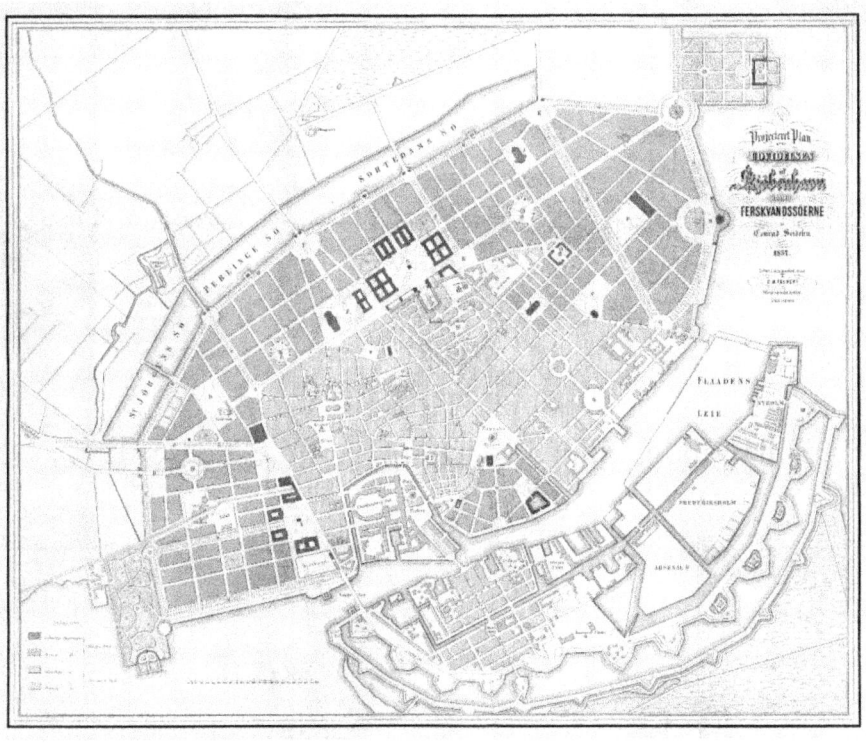

Illustration 54

Response:

_____
_____
_____
_____
_____

5. What do you think is in this picture?

COMPOUND SURFACE CONDENSER WITH AIR AND CIRCULATING PUMPS.

Illustration 55

Response:

_____

_____

_____

_____

_____

6. The effects of industrialization on what industry are shown below?

Illustration 56

Response: _____

7. What was the purpose of this late 1800s Danish building?

Illustration 57

Response:

_____
_____
_____
_____
_____

8. Which social class do you think the person from the picture belonged to?

Illustration 58

Response: _____

9. What middle-class values can you identify in this picture?

Illustration 59

Response:

_____

_____

_____

_____

_____

10. This person is an example of how people in Denmark could grow and advance through education during the intense industrialization and urbanization period. Who is he?

Illustration 60

Response: _____

Multiple Choice Questions

1. Which Danish city became known as the "Manchester of Denmark" due to its thriving textile industry during the Industrial Revolution?

    A. Copenhagen

    B. Vejle

    C. Brede

    D. Valby

2. What was the name of the Danish social reformer who advocated for improved living and working conditions for industrial workers?

    A. Orla Lehmann

    B. Peter Rochegune Munch

    C. Carl Theodor Zahle

    D. Jørgen Jørgensen

3. Besides textiles, which industry played a crucial role in Denmark's economic development during the Industrial Revolution?

    A. Shipbuilding

    B. Food processing and production

    C. Paper

    D. Dairy

4. What role did education play in Denmark's industrial development?

    A. None at all

    B. A small role

    C. A major role

    D. It played a role in some industries

5. How did the introduction of constitutional monarchy help the country's growth and urbanization?

    A. By erasing shipping privileges

    B. Guaranteeing the right of ownership

    C. Establishing contractual freedom and freedom of association

    D. All of the above

6. How did Danish farmers deal with the Industrial Revolution?
    A. They looked to use the new technologies to their advantage
    B. They resisted using the new technologies
    C. They only accepted some of the new technologies
    D. They wanted to use the new technologies but didn't know how

7. Who was the Danish inventor who drastically improved the dairy industry?
    A. Ole Johansen Winstrup
    B. Wilhelm Hellesen
    C. Emil Christian Hansen
    D. Lars Christian Nielsen

8. Which Danish city saw the largest rise in industrial production?
    A. Aalborg
    B. Copenhagen
    C. Randers
    D. Odense

9. What motivated the growth of industrialization?
    A. Higher need to export
    B. Higher demand on the Danish market
    C. Taxes
    D. Lack of reforms

10. Which other sectors did the industrialized agriculture industry help grow in the late 19th century?
    A. Finance
    B. Transport
    C. Trade
    D. All of the above

True or False

1. The introduction of steam-powered machinery revolutionized Danish agriculture during the 19th century.
   - True
   - False

2. The Danish government implemented child labor laws to regulate the employment of children in factories during the 19th century.
   - True
   - False

3. Denmark started to use import taxes when transport costs became higher across Europe.
   - True
   - False

4. By 1940, more Danes were employed in industry than in agriculture.
   - True
   - False

5. Between 1870 and 1914, Denmark had larger economic growth than any other European country.
   - True
   - False

6. The loss of Schleswig-Holstein territories also contributed to the need for industrialization.
   - True
   - False

7. Railway construction only added to the industry costs in Denmark.
   - True
   - False

8. The industrial growth and urbanization of Denmark was an easy and strong process.
   - True
   - False

9. The thriving banking industry also played a role in speeding up the

industrial revolution.
- True
- False

10. Aalborg was the first Danish city to have a fully industrial and urban society.
- True
- False

Chapter 7: World War Woes: Danish Neutrality Tested

When the world was shaken by two wars, life in Denmark changed drastically. During World War I, Denmark remained neutral, but this came at an enormous price. Then came the German occupation, which brought the already struggling Danish economy to the floor. This chapter brings you questions about the impact of wartime shortages on Danish society, the German occupation of Denmark, resistance efforts, and more.

Multiple Choice Questions

1. Why was Denmark's neutrality threatened during World War I?
    A. Due to its position
    B. Due to its size
    C. Due to its closeness to Germany
    D. Due to its past conflicts with Great Britain

2. Which was the largest naval battle fought in World War I, and why did it threaten Denmark's neutrality?
    A. Battle of Heligoland Bight
    B. Battle of Jutland
    C. Battle of the Dogger Bank
    D. The First Battle of the Marne

3. How did the warring countries play a role in Denmark's ability to remain neutral during World War I?

    A. They used less pressure than expected

    B. They didn't come close to Denmark's waters

    C. They underestimated each other

    D. They wanted to resolve the conflict quickly

4. What was the only period when that war came close to Danish territories?

    A. When the British ships wanted to enter Denmark's side of the Baltic Sea

    B. When Germany launched a submarine war

    C. When the Russians were chasing the Germans near Danish waters

    D. None of the above

5. Why was the war conflict between Germany and the United Kingdom so harmful to the Danish economy?

    A. They were Denmark's main export market

    B. They had access to useful trading routes

    C. They wanted to take over Denmark and rob its supplies

    D. They wouldn't provide Denmark with metals, coal, and other necessary resources it didn't have

6. What was the most harmful result of the difficult trade with Britain and Germany?

    A. Ships were lost at sea

    B. Shortage of goods

    C. Too much animal products

    D. Lower inflation

7. How did some people take advantage of the food shortages?

    A. By falsely advertising trade opportunities

    B. By pretending to help others but taking their money

    C. By selling products at higher prices

    D. By selling cheap products with suspicious origins

8. What was the result of the inflation during World War I?
   A. Increased cost of living
   B. Increased rent prices
   C. Too low income for those on a fixed income
   D. All of the above

9. When did the state start to help people suffering from the effects of inflation and loss of trade?
   A. During the third year of the war
   B. During the first year of the war
   C. During the second year of the war
   D. By the end of the war

10. How did the public react to the first decision of the Extraordinary Commission?
   A. Everyone was happy with the decision
   B. No one was happy with the decision
   C. Small farmers and buyers were happy with the decision
   D. Only the large producers were happy with the decision

Identify the Picture

1. Who is in this picture?

Illustration 61

Response: _____

2. Identify the building from the picture.

Illustration 62

Response: _____

3. Who is in this picture?

Illustration 63

Response:

_____
_____
_____
_____
_____

4. What is in this picture?

Freikorps Danmark

Illustration 64

Response:

_____
_____
_____
_____
_____

5. The pictured event had a major role in Denmark's capitulation under the German advance. What was this event?

Illustration 65

Response:

_____

_____

_____

_____

_____

6. What is the name of the Danish territory above the bold line in the middle?

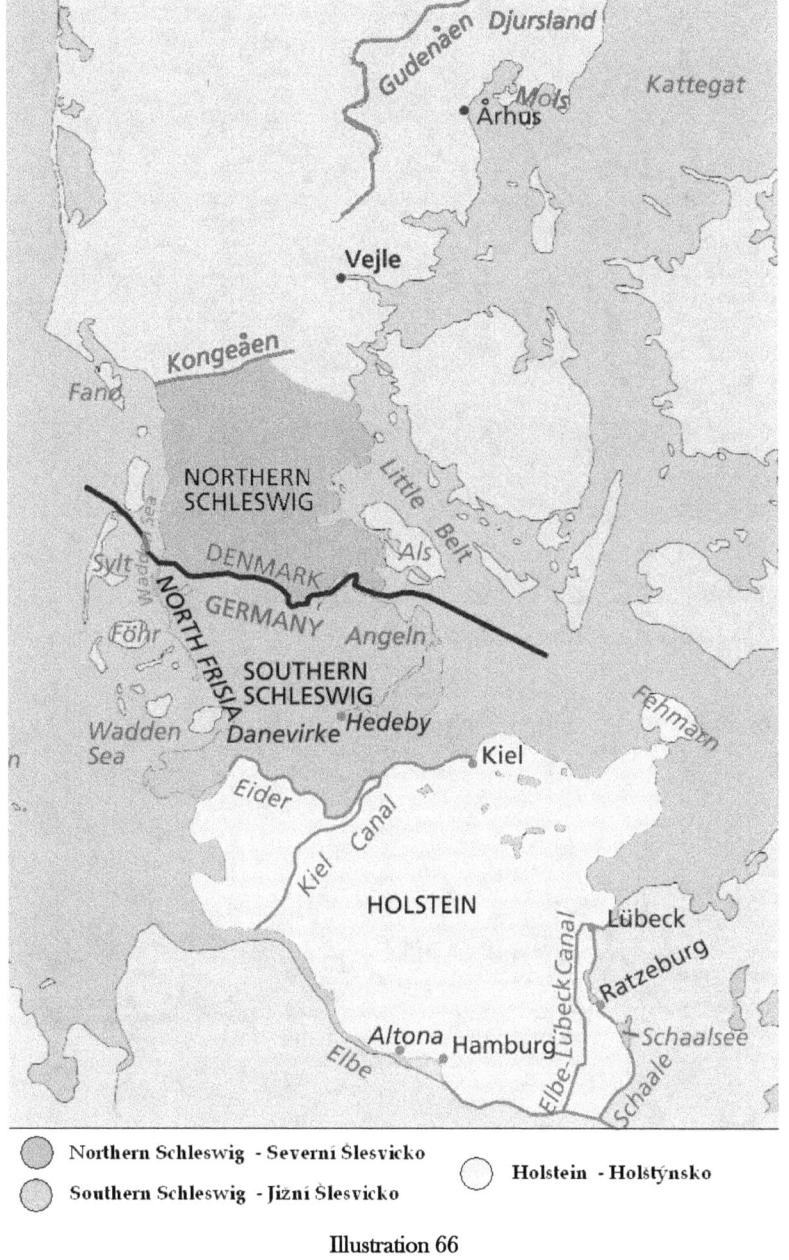

Illustration 66

Response: _____

7. What is in the picture?

Illustration 67

Response: _____

8. What is the name of this ship?

Illustration 68

Response: _____

9. In whose honor was this plaque made?

CETTE EGLISE SERVIT D'HOPITAL
AU LENDEMAIN DE LA BATAILLE

DU 18 JUIN 1815

CHARITABLEMENT LES BRAINOIS
VINRENT EN AIDE AUX BLESSES

Illustration 69

Response:

_____

_____

_____

_____

_____

10. What former Danish territory is pictured here?

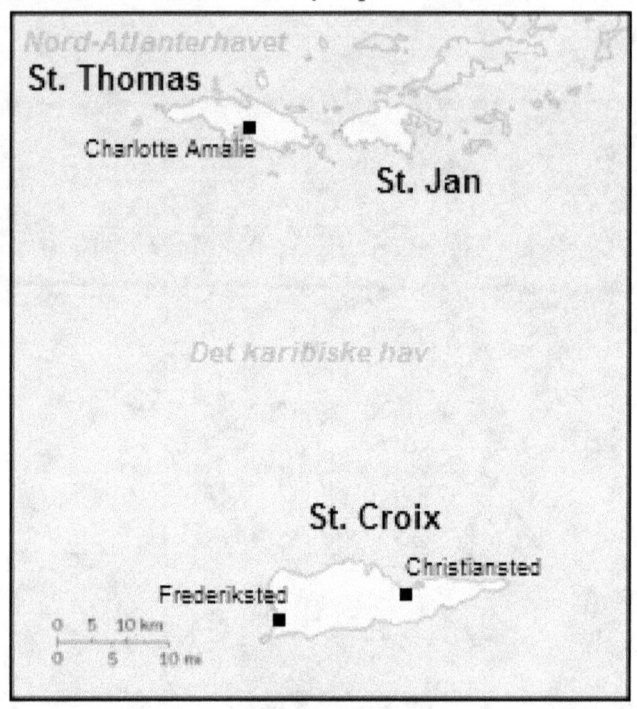

Illustration 70

Response: _____

Fill in the Blanks

1. The dissatisfied workers tried to seek help by joining
   ....

2. On 7 August 1914, the Danish parliament passed the
   ...., which allowed the interior minister to
   regulate food prices and trade with countries.

3. The Venstre was a .... against the ....

4. Food rationing was introduced when shortages became greater in
   ....

5. According to Social Liberals, rationing should've been a starting
   point for a more equal distribution of ...., while Venstre said
   that it should be .... after the war.

6. By the end of the war, the previously stronger farmers'
   organizations now faced a ...., who were ready
   to defend their wages and fight for ....

7. To make the inflation less noticeable, the workers managed to get
   triple wages, but the employers often retaliated
   by...

8. During the last years of World War I, the Danish state tried to
   manage its finances by ....

9. Even during World War I, neutrality became stretched out to the
   .... direction.

10. The Tune Stronghold (a series of fortifications from Køge Bay to
    Roskilde Fjord guarded by 50,000 troops) was set up to
    ....

True or False

1. Danish workers had eight-hour workdays before World War I.
   - True
   - False

2. The Danish state did not pay for extra security forces to prevent people from being cheated out of their money.
   - True
   - False

3. The diseases caused by poverty only affected children and the very old.
   - True
   - False

4. The states used the loan money to invest in production.
   - True
   - False

5. The investors bought large stocks of produce for export to the Baltic Region and were able to sell them at good prices.
   - True
   - False

6. The international recession in 1920 further hurt the Danish economy.
   - True
   - False

7. The Danish working week during and after World War I had 40 hours.
   - True
   - False

8. By World War II, Denmark had given up on being neutral.
   - True
   - False

9. The German occupation of Denmark lasted five years.
   - True
   - False

10. When the Freedom Council began the resistance efforts, Denmark was at war with Germany.
    • True
    • False

Reflection Questions

1. Why did Denmark choose to stay neutral during World War I, and how did this decision affect the country?

   _____

   _____

   _____

   _____

   _____

2. What was the name of the crisis agreement that helped stabilize Denmark's economy between the two world wars?

   _____

   _____

   _____

   _____

   _____

3. What was the only air attack that threatened Denmark's neutrality during World War I?

   _____

   _____

   _____

   _____

4. What was a German water-based action that harmed Danish neutrality and economy?

   _____

   _____

   _____

   _____

   _____

5. During World War I, some Danish soldiers fought under German command despite the country's neutrality. Why?

_____

_____

_____

_____

_____

6. How did the Germans control the Danish economy and government even before the occupation?

_____

_____

_____

_____

_____

7. How did life change for Danish citizens during World War II under German occupation? What were some ways people resisted

_____

_____

_____

_____

_____

8. Can you name a few brave individuals who led the Danish resistance against the Germans? What did they do to resist?

_____

_____

_____

_____

_____

9. How did underground newspapers and secret operations help the Danish resistance movement during the war?

_____

_____

_____

_____

_____

10. What were some important moments that led to Denmark's freedom from German rule? How did Danish people celebrate?

_____

_____

_____

_____

_____

Chapter 8: WW2: Denmark's Resistance and Resilience

By the time the Germans reached Denmark's borders, the Danes knew that they would gain more by surrendering willingly. They were promised support and the opportunity to maintain their neutrality – none of which they got. So, they started resisting, leading a strong movement that surprised even the powerful Nazi forces. Here are your chances to learn more about the Danish resistance fighters and networks.

Match the Figures

Match the key figures in the Danish resistance movement and their contributions to the fight against the Germans.

1. Mogens Fog	Leader of Eigil, a subgroup of Holger Danske. Known for capturing German collaborators.
2. Monica Wichfeld	A Canadian-borne Danish sailor, he used his sailing skills to transport weapons to the resistance groups.
3. Ellen Christensen	Member and parachute commander of the Freedom Council. Known for sabotaging bridges, railways, factories,

	and German military bases in Denmark.
4. Povl Falk-Jensen	He is often called Flammen (flaming) after his bright red hair. Together with Citronen, he made the most famous resistance duo in Denmark.
5. Knud Pedersen	Doctor and member of the Danish Freedom Council. Founded the Frit Danmark, the resistance newspaper.
6. Kim Malthe-Bruun	Raised funds for printing the underground newspapers and stored explosives, firearms, and ammunition for the resistance members.
7. Ole Lippmann	Known under the codename of Citronen. Participated in the bombing of the Forum Copenhagen.
8. Jørgen Haagen Schmith	Daughter of Knud Mogensen and a journalist who contributed to several youth resistance journals in 1942 and 1943.
9. Bent Faurschou Hviid	Artist, resistance leader, and founder of the Churchill Club (he was 17 at the time).
10. Lone Maslocha	Worked as a nurse at Bispebjerg Hospital, where she distributed underground newspapers. She also hid Danish Jews until they could be safely transported to Sweden.

Identify the Pictures

1. Can you guess who built this vehicle?

Illustration 71

Response: _____

2. Identify this person.

Illustration 72

Response: _____

3. Can you spot the fight in this picture?

Illustration 73

Response:

_____

_____

_____

_____

_____

4. Which major resistance group did these Danes belong to?

Illustration 74

Response: _____

5. People as young as school age were resistance members. Which group do these boys belong to?

Illustration 75

Response: _____

6. Who is in the picture?

Illustration 76

Response: _____

7. This was the logo of which resistant-related party?

Illustration 77

Response: _____

8. This was the collar tab of which organization.

Illustration 78

Response: _____

9. What is in this picture?

Illustration 79

Response:

_____
_____
_____
_____
_____

10. After liberation, Denmark was full of celebrations, but also of events like this. Do you know what event this was?

Illustration 80

Response:

_____
_____
_____
_____
_____

True or False

1. In 1943, the underground network helped 8,000 people to safety.
   - True
   - False

2. The rescue of the Jews was organized.
   - True
   - False

3. Resistance members had lookouts in the harbors to see when it was safe for them and the Jews to pass.
   - True
   - False

4. The occupation retaliated against the resistance movement.
   - True
   - False

5. In 1945, the resistance group was preparing to forcefully take back control.
   - True
   - False

6. The Social Democrats were in danger of losing the leadership after the war.
   - True
   - False

7. In 1943, strikes and sabotage caused the end of cooperation between the German administration and the Danish government.
   - True
   - False

8. By the end of 1943, the German authorities disarmed the Danish army and navy.
   - True
   - False

9. The Danish police force remained in place during the occupation.
   - True
   - False

10. The resistance movement became so strong that the Germans had to bring in the Gestapo to fight it.
    - True
    - False

Fill in the Blanks

1. Even before World War II, the Danish government asked the press to stop criticizing Germany and Nazism to ....

2. In mid-April 1940, Danish army intelligence officers known as .... were reporting to London allies.

3. When Germany offered Denmark a reciprocal non-aggression pact in ...., most Danish political parties agreed to sign it.

4. The German invasion of Denmark in April 1940 was ....

5. Initially, the Germans agreed to let Denmark remain an ....

6. As time went on, all remaining .... collaborated with the Germans more and more.

7. After their victories in Belgium, Holland, Luxembourg, and France in ...., the Germans started to make changes in the Danish government and leadership.

8. The new government leader, Erik Scavenius, encouraged the Danes to work toward a .... and collaboration with a ....

9. At Germany's "advice," the .... was banned.

10. In 1941, Denmark joined the Anti-Comintern Pact, an ....

Reflection Questions

1. What were some of the ways Danish citizens resisted the German occupation during World War II?

   _____

   _____

   _____

   _____

   _____

2. How did the Danish resistance use sabotage and covert operations to disrupt German activities?

   _____

   _____

   _____

   _____

   _____

3. Describe the role of underground newspapers and communication networks in spreading information and coordinating resistance efforts.

   _____

   _____

   _____

   _____

   _____

4. What were the challenges faced by Danish resistance fighters, and how did they overcome them?

   _____

   _____

   _____

   _____

5. Where did the resistance members get help for their operations?

_____

_____

_____

_____

_____

6. What were the most hated symbols of Nazi oppression?

_____

_____

_____

_____

_____

7. What were some of the benefits of the German occupation?

_____

_____

_____

_____

_____

8. What were some of the dilemmas faced by those who collaborated with the Germans?

_____

_____

_____

_____

_____

9. The resistance groups' efforts were rooted in different values. What were these?

_____

_____

_____

_____

_____

10. The cooperation with the Germans helped control the economy, but the people still weren't satisfied. Why?

_____

_____

_____

_____

_____

Chapter 9: Rebuilding and Reforming Denmark Post-War

After the German occupation, the Danes became wealthier and received more jobs, education, social support, and growth opportunities than ever before. If you want to learn how they recovered their economy and achieved an extraordinary social welfare state, don't miss out on this chapter about the rebuilding of Denmark post-war.

True or False

1. Denmark refused to collaborate with Germany after liberation.
   - True
   - False
2. During the postwar era, Denmark's population quickly began to increase.
   - True
   - False
3. Public health improved after World War II.
   - True
   - False

4. The new foreign labor force, which began to seep into Denmark in the 1960s, was a controversial issue.
   - True
   - False

5. A common Nordic labor market was introduced after World War II.
   - True
   - False

6. The German occupation forces remained in one part of Denmark.
   - True
   - False

7. Denmark's post-war progress has slowed down but wasn't completely prevented by the Cold War.
   - True
   - False

8. Post-war Danes lived in small houses.
   - True
   - False

9. Central heating became popular during the 1960s.
   - True
   - False

10. It was also more modern.
    - True
    - False

Fill in the Blanks

1. In the 1960s, Denmark went through a decade of ...., which helped establish the modern ....

2. By the 1960s, the .... sector became the largest contributor to the state income.

3. By 1972, only 10% of the active workforce worked in ...., but there were more people earning wages as .... or.......................................

4. The opposition believed that the welfare state was .... because it would make people rely on benefits too much and ... .

5. The Danish welfare state was based on .... values, as most countries from this region started introducing the system around the same time.

6. The welfare system was financed from .... and not .... as in other European countries.

7. The state pension as a universal benefit was introduced in ....

8. The established welfare policy led to the building of many new hospitals and care homes for the .... and ....

9. In the early 1970s, the Economic Council created two plans to set a sustainable .... for welfare expenses.

10. Every Danish person's health care, social security, education, voting, and military service rights were tracked by the .... system.

Multiple Choice Questions

1. What year was the Central Person Register (CPR) introduced?
    A. 1958
    B. 1968
    C. 1970
    D. 1962

2. When was sales tax first introduced in Denmark?
    A. 1967
    B. 1959
    C. 1956
    D. 1955

3. As part of the sustainable budgeting for the welfare state, taxes were increased...
    A. Quickly
    B. Every year
    C. Every five years
    D. Gradually, over three decades

4. How many tiers did the local government have after the post-war municipal reforms?
    A. Two
    B. Three
    C. Five
    D. Seven

5. Besides a better welfare system, the economy also required the state to find lands for what purposes?
    A. Agriculture
    B. Workers homes
    C. Industrial districts
    D. Green spaces

6. Which group of Danish citizens benefited from the new welfare state?

    A. The working force

    B. The elderly

    C. People of all ages

    D. Students

7. What concept was removed from the new welfare policy?

    A. Deserving needy

    B. Equal deserving

    C. Status-based need

    D. Need for rights

8. What part of agriculture developed the most post-war?

    A. Farm labor

    B. Industrial

    C. Livestock farming

    D. Fertilizer use

9. Why was growing agriculture quickly important for the Danish economy?

    A. To supply the Danish market

    B. To keep up with the population growth

    C. To use fewer workers in farms and more in urban factories

    D. To produce more animal products for export

10. Which was a new challenge in the welfare state?

    A. Funding

    B. Getting people to accept it

    C. People living longer

    D. Greater need for benefits

Identify the Picture

1. What do you think was the purpose of this building during the Danish welfare state?

Illustration 81

Response:

_____

_____

_____

_____

_____

2. Identify the person from the picture.

Illustration 82

Response: _____

3. Which members of the alliance are shown (in dark blue) in this picture?

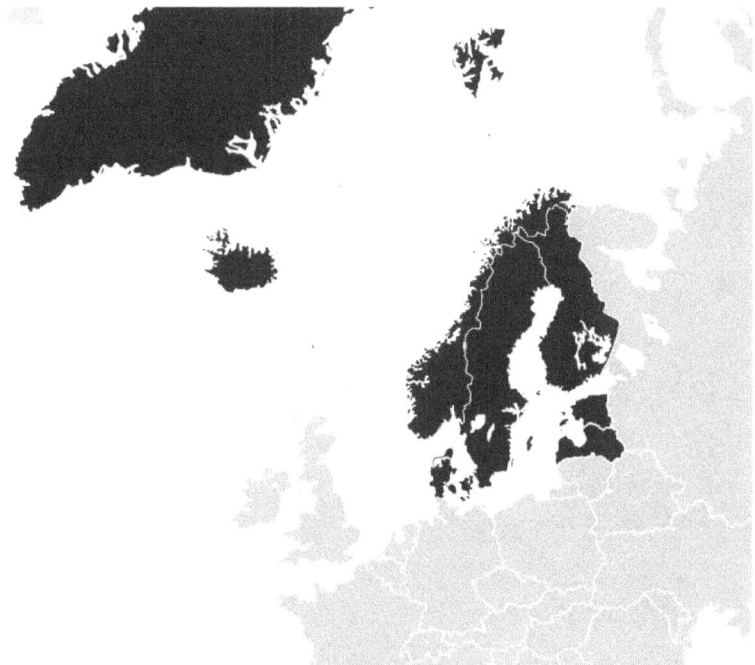

Illustration 83

Response: _____

4. What does this map depict?

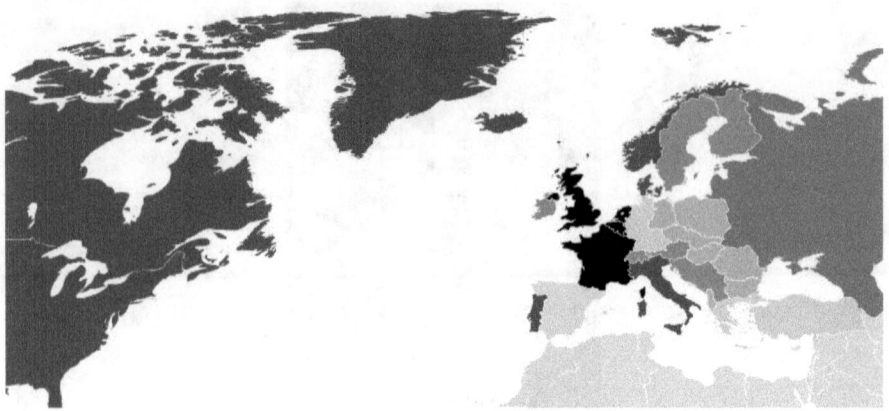

Illustration 84

Response:

_____

_____

_____

_____

_____

5. Why did this organization hinder Denmark's efforts to rebuild its economy?

Illustration 85

Response:

_____
_____
_____
_____
_____

6. Identify the person in the picture.

Illustration 86

Response: _____

7. In 1957, Denmark signed a treaty to gain access to European markets and establish common trade customs. What was the name of this treaty?

Illustration 87

Response: _____

8. Adopting a U.S.-based plan made a huge difference in Danish welfare. What plan was this?

Whatever the weather
We only reach welfare
together

Illustration 88

Response:

_____
_____
_____
_____
_____

9. Where do you think this picture was taken?

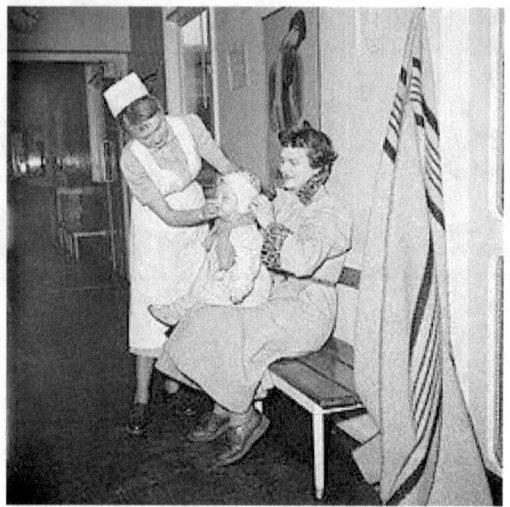

Illustration 89

Response: _____

10. What is in this picture?

Illustration 90

Response: _____

Reflection Questions

1. How did Denmark rebuild its economy and infrastructure in the aftermath of World War II?

   _____

   _____

   _____

   _____

   _____

2. What were some of the key social welfare initiatives introduced in post-war Denmark, and how did they improve the lives of citizens?

   _____

   _____

   _____

   _____

   _____

3. Describe the advancements made in gender equality and women's rights during Denmark's post-war period.

   _____

   _____

   _____

   _____

   _____

4. Discuss the significance of Denmark's establishment as a modern welfare state. How did it differ from pre-war Denmark?

   _____

   _____

   _____

   _____

   _____

5. What role did education play in Denmark's post-war progress, and how did it contribute to the nation's development?

_____

_____

_____

_____

_____

6. What caused the changes in the population patterns?

_____

_____

_____

_____

_____

7. How did the modern welfare state support people's happiness?

_____

_____

_____

_____

_____

8. Besides urban workers, agricultural workers also relied on welfare benefits. Why?

_____

_____

_____

_____

_____

9. How did the trade, transport, and services sector outgrow agriculture and some industry sectors?

_____

_____

_____

_____

_____

10. Which municipal reform contributed to the welfare state the most?

_____

_____

_____

_____

_____

Chapter 10: Modern Danish Innovation and Cultural Evolution

Modern Denmark is known as the land of innovations, cultural dynamism, and sustainable development. Besides being a country deeply committed to environmental responsibility, Denmark is also big on nurturing education, culture, and traditions. Scientists, artists, architects, and entrepreneurs blend the new with the old, showcasing Denmark's progressive society that thrives after many challenges. This chapter will give you the opportunity to learn about or test your knowledge of Danish innovators and innovations.

True or False

1. Danish culture is based on trust.
   - True
   - False
2. The Danes don't like to volunteer.
   - True
   - False

3. The Danes drive their bicycles even to social events.

- True
- False

4. The Danish innovators are a result of living in a country with few resources.
    - True
    - False

5. Denmark has a low number of innovators compared to its population.
    - True
    - False

6. The Danes are one of the happiest people in the world.
    - True
    - False

7. Denmark has many modern restaurants.
    - True
    - False

8. Education is free in Denmark.
    - True
    - False

9. Danes have an excellent work-life balance.
    - True
    - False

10. Danish culture became more diverse after World War II.
    - True
    - False

Identify the Picture

1. What do you think those lines are in the water?

Illustration 91

Response:

_____

_____

_____

_____

_____

2. What is so unique about this building?

Illustration 92

Response:

_____

_____

_____

_____

_____

3. What's the name of the Danish Island that's completely sustainable?

Illustration 93

Response: _____

4. Name the designer of this chair.

Illustration 94

Response: _____

5. Danish architects also left their mark on buildings and historical landmarks outside Denmark. Do you know who designed this building?

Illustration 95

Response: _____

6. What is the person honored by this sign famous for?

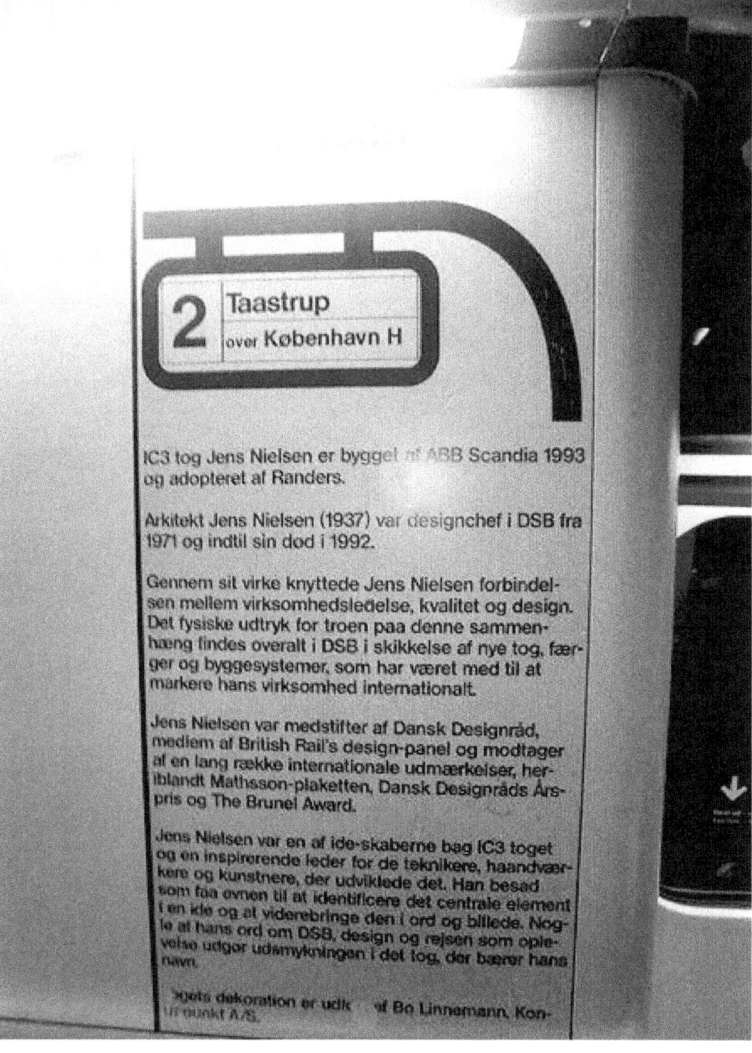

Illustration 96

Response:

_____

_____

_____

_____

_____

7. Do you see something unusual about this bridge?

Illustration 97

Response:

_____

_____

_____

_____

_____

8. Could you guess what this structure is used for?

Illustration 98

Response:

_____
_____
_____
_____
_____

9. Whose artwork is this?

Illustration 99

Response: _____

10. This Danish scientist embodies the core Danish values. Do you know why?

Illustration 100

Response:

_____
_____
_____
_____
_____

Fill in the Blanks

1. A good work-life balance, a positive work culture, and support for family life make Danish people ....

2. Danish chef Brian Mark Hansen won the Bocuse d'Or contest, which is known as ....

3. When the Danes say hygge, they mean ....

4. To the Danes, sustainability means using renewable energy, ..., green transportation, and ....

5. Denmark's effort to invest in sustainable energy is particularly admirable because the country requires .... for more than half a year.

6. Denmark operates the world's first carbon neutral ....

7. Denmark's ecosystems are so clean that the Danes can .... anywhere in the country.

8. Denmark is known for activism for .... across the world.

9. Jussi Adler-Olsen is one of the world's most famous ....

10. Smilla's Sense of Snow is a movie based on the novel by ....

Reflection Questions

1. Which Danish company pioneered wind energy technology and has since become a global leader in sustainable energy solutions?

_____

_____

_____

_____

_____

2. Which Danish inventor and entrepreneur is renowned for creating a popular construction toy system in the 20th century, inspiring creativity and innovation in children worldwide?

_____

_____

_____

_____

_____

3. Which is the primary, environmentally friendly mode of transportation in modern Denmark?

_____

_____

_____

_____

_____

4. What is the largest source of bioenergy in Denmark?

_____

_____

_____

_____

_____

5. In Denmark, even district (or central) heating is often fueled by renewable energy sources. Which one is used besides biomass and wind?

_____

_____

_____

_____

_____

6. What does the term "first fuel" mean, and why is it important for Danish energy consumption?

_____

_____

_____

_____

_____

7. What Danish company is the fifth biggest dairy manufacturer in the world and the largest one in Scandinavia?

_____

_____

_____

_____

_____

8. Which Danish company is the world leader in water control system production?

_____

_____

_____

_____

_____

9. Which Danish cities have become the center of the robotics industry?

_____

_____

_____

_____

_____

10. What 1990s event led to the improvement in Denmark's telecommunication system?

_____

_____

_____

_____

_____

Matching Trivia

1. Holger Møller Hansen	Designed the first drum motor used for industrial purposes in the 1950s.
2. Peter L. Jensen	First manufactured insulin in 1922.
3. Lars and Jens Rasmussen	Danish athlete who formed the rules and invented the modern sport of handball.
4. Susanne Koefoed	Danish-Canadian designer who coined the term "Copenhagenization" to describe the Danish capital's unique biking lifestyle and urban infrastructure.
5. John Kirkegaard	In 1951, he invented fiber-optic imaging, the technology that transfers images to the eye with optical fibers. It's used for endoscopes.
6. Elise Sørensen	Entrepreneur and co-founder of Skype.
7. August Krogh	In 1915, he invented the speaker while experimenting with wireless telephone systems.
8. Holger Nielsen	A nurse who designed the first ostomy system (stoma bag).
9. Mikael Colville-Andersen	The Danish student who designed and first used the International Symbol of Access (ISA) to signify a place reserved for people with disabilities in 1968.
10. Janus Friis	Invented Google Maps while working at Where 2 Technologies in the early 2000s.

Answer Key

Chapter 1

Multiple Choice Questions

1. D. The Viking ships were used not only in raids and warfare but also for exploring new lands they could settle on and trading goods with other nations.

2. A. The Vikings mostly used oak for building their vessels because it was the most durable type of wood. Oak is resistant to saltwater, harsh weather conditions, and even demanding battle maneuvers.

3. D. Leif Ericson, a brave Viking explorer, is believed to have reached the shores of North America around 1000, more than 500 years before Christopher Columbus set foot on the continent.

4. B. The Vikings' ships were made durable due to the clinker technique. Clinkering means overlapping planks and riveting them together. This creates a flexible and incredibly strong hull, making it easier to conquer challenging sea conditions. While it was first used on longships, the technique became so successful that the Vikings decided to adapt and continue using it on other types of ships.

5. D. The intricate carvings on the Viking ships had several purposes. As the number of ships leaving for exploring, raiding, and trading grew, it was necessary to distinguish the ships. When the enemy or friend saw who was approaching, they knew to prepare for either battle or friendly greeting. However, the Vikings were also big on

symbolism and believed that certain symbols (like dragon heads, for example) could ward off evil spirits – so they put these on their boats.

6. A. While the Vikings made different ships, each tailored to specific purposes, the two main types they used were narrow warships and wide cargo vessels. The small size of the warships was better for easy maneuvering (like escape and attack). Meanwhile, the cargo ships had to be larger and sturdier so they wouldn't buckle under the weight of the merchandise they were transporting.

7. C. The keel was a fundamental part of a Viking ship. One of the reasons their vessels were so stable and easy to maneuver when changing directions is that they used a unique keel construction method. They started putting more work into keel building after the second half of the 8th century.

8. B. Despite their larger size, Viking trade ships could handle anything. Moreover, because the Vikings traveled great distances, they were able to transport anything from spices to metals to textiles and even slaves.

9. A. Viking ships, especially knarrs, which were used for transporting cargo, were secure enough to deter raiders. Their interiors often had different designs to make transporting products of various shapes and sizes easier. Lastly, they were made by experienced sailors who knew what helped ships navigate accurately and safely.

10. D. From the 9th century onward, the Vikings focused on building narrower vessels, especially for the longships they used for trading and exploring. These allowed them to sail both shallow rivers and open seas. They also began to use larger, square sails, which were better at catching the wind. This made their ships faster and more durable on longer journeys.

Did You Know?

The clinker technique is still used in boat building, serving as a legacy of Viking shipbuilding techniques.

True or False I :

1. False. The longships were mainly used for exploring and raiding. For trading, the Vikings had knarrs, which were wide and massive

vessels.

2. False. The Vikings were experts in finding shipworthy woods locally and didn't need to buy them from other places.

3. False. Viking ships were very easy to repair. If they were damaged, the builders were able to get them up and running in no time.

4. True. Knarrs were used for transporting large amounts of cargo, which sometimes included livestock and other shipments that needed a lot of room.

5. True. The Vikings used many new designs, including narrower hulls for their longships, which made their ships faster than ever.

6. True. Another innovation the Vikings created was the unique oar placement in the airport, which made the ships easier to navigate in tight spaces or risky situations.

7. False. Unlike previous shipbuilders, the Vikings also thought of using rudders mounted on the starboard side, making their vessel easier to steer.

8. True. The Vikings' culture always included elements of the maritime lifestyle, and this was also seen in their shipbuilding.

9. False. Viking explorers sailed to many parts of the world many years before the Europeans.

10. False. The first raid on English shores happened at the end of the 8th century.

Did You Know?

As they started to expand their horizons, the Vikings found many thriving cities and monasteries on the coastal area of the continent. Due to their isolation and defenseless inhabitants, these turned out to be easy targets.

Find the Match

1. Family lineage, job title, and wealth – The order of Viking social structure.

2. Jarls – Rulers and nobility.

3. Karls – Craftsmen and free peasants.

4. Thralls – Slaves.

5. Chiefs and leaders – Kings governing the military and important jarls.

6. Lesser leaders - People who lead the ceremonies and religious events.

7. Berserkers —Trained Viking warriors who fought as if they were in a trance.

8. Shieldmaidens - Female community protectors and additional helpers in raids.

9. Slaves - Prisoners of war and people fallen into debt.

10. Viking - A term used for those who went on raids.

Did You Know?

When they started to venture beyond Western Europe, the Vikings slowly began to settle and take up trading and farming in their new homelands. Their voyages, accompanied by a reign of terror, soon became history. The favorable climate outside Scandinavia also made farming easier, so there was no need to continue the seafaring warrior lifestyle.

Identify the Picture

1. The Oseberg Ship. An excellent example of Viking shipbuilding skills, the ship was discovered in a burial bound in Norway. It was built in the early 9th century and has a clinker hull, a carved prow, and a skeletal construction, where the frame is built first. Then, using the frame as a guide, the rest of the planks are attached to it to create the hull.

2. The unique kite bow of Viking ships. This one has curling iron pieces that look like a dragon's mane, which was often used for protection and to make the vessel look scarier.

3. The Ladbyskibet is a slightly newer ship model. It was found in Denmark and was likely made in the 10th century. Its longer but narrower body makes it easier to adapt to long travels and heavy loads.

4. This Knarr, Snorri, was the first to recreate Leif Erikson's voyage from Greenland to Newfoundland. It had the same (and, by its time, much older) navigational tools that were used by sailors before the Viking era. Yet, on the second attempt, it led the crew to their destination, proving the Viking's excellent navigational skills.

5. The picture shows how complex Viking trade routes were in Medieval times - and this was only in Northwest Europe! They

built similar connections in all directions across the world.

6. These are all objects used in wartime, which shows how important raiding and war were in Viking societies. From swords and spears to scissors and harness hooks, you can see everything you might think a warrior needs when going to battle.

7. These items show that displaying lineage, title, wealth, and societal roles through clothes and accessories was also important to the Vikings. Unlike the horned helmets shown in modern Viking-inspired art, they wore bronze and silver brooches, pendants, and rings and carried decorative amulets, ingots, keys, combs, etc.

8. This beaker was found in a rich Viking woman's grave. According to historians, glass beakers were often used in ceremonies led by women from important families.

9. This figure shows a Viking-age woman armed with a sword or spear and holding a shield. The woman is known as a Valkyrie and was found on the Isle of Fyn, Hårby, Denmark.

10. The name of the assembly was Thing or Folkmoot. Here, every free member of the Viking community could gather and speak about important matters, vote, and make decisions about everything from explorations to raids to defense to farming. It's a unique place that shows how important equality and justice were to the Vikings.

Did You Know?

The Vikings' sturdy ships allowed them to trade not only on the British Isles but also toward North Africa and the Mediterranean. The more their shipbuilding improved, the more they were able to expand their trade. This means getting more goods and getting to know different cultures. Through their voyages, Vikings not only traded goods but also stories, technologies, and practices with the people they encountered.

True or False II

1. False. The horns you see on Viking helmets in movies and media are the product of fiction. The ancient Vikings didn't have horns and other protruding items on them.

2. True. In addition to their handy tools, Vikings navigated the seas and rivers using the stars and their own experience.

3. True. In Viking society, women were able to participate in raids, vote, trade, and become important leaders. Likewise, men also

helped out in households and farms.

4. False. Besides those born into important families, Vikings who proved they were brave, hardworking, and worked with others could also become leaders.

5. False. While many thralls came from foreign lands, some Vikings also became slaves after losing their status, money, and support.

6. True. The attack on Lindisfarne was the first of many raids the Vikings made on monasteries across Europe.

7. True. The religious leaders believed the attack to be a punishment for an unknown sin and ordered the monks to stop doing anything that would be seen as a sin to avoid further attack.

8. False. The main reason the Vikings began to raid monasteries on the British shores was that these were easier to access. They often had prized items the Vikings could trade to obtain what they needed.

9. False. Once they realized the Vikings were after the treasures hidden in monasteries, the British started secretly moving these items to safer places to better prepare for the attacks.

10. True. The Viking raids changed not only how the other European warriors prepared for the attacks but also how they viewed the Vikings. They were previously seen as primitive people, but now Europe realized how smart and innovative they can be.

Chapter 2

Multiple Choice Questions

1. A. Kronborg Castle was built by Frederik II between 1574 and 1585 as a symbol of his wealth, which was obtained after Eric of Pomerania built Krogen. This fortress controlled the entrance to Oresund, and the king collected large dues from the passing ships.

2. D. The purpose of the Medieval tournament was to showcase the knight's courage, skills, and strength. However, it also served as a training exercise for the knights – not to mention a form of entertainment for the people.

3. C. Ogier The Dane, one of Denmark's most famous heroes, is mentioned in the medieval epic poem "The Heroic Ballads." While little is known about his origins, he was believed to be one of Charlemagne's military leaders.

4. B. The Kronborg Castle was destroyed twice. First, it was set on fire in 1629. Christian IV rebuilt it with extensive new Baroque decorations. However, in 1656, the Swedes bombed the castle. The Swedes occupied the remains and the art pieces that hadn't been destroyed previously.

5. C. In medieval Denmark, very few people could read and write. They used images and symbols to communicate, express their culture, and connect with others. However, those who could read and write also had more expensive art pieces, which they used to display their status.

6. D. Besides the members of the royal family, many landowners also gained the status of nobility in Medieval Denmark. The country's main income came from agriculture, which meant that those who owned lands had power. They multiplied this power by serving in the king's military service, which meant they didn't have to pay taxes after their lands.

7. A. Forming towns were very popular in Denmark during the Middle Ages. As the population grew, people needed more places to trade, gather to discuss important matters, show their arts and crafts, etc., so they started forming towns. Most of the modern towns you'll find today in the country were created during the Medieval period – and some are just as colorful as they were back in the day.

8. B. Christian IV is known as the king of building the most magnificent structures in Denmark. Granted, he became king when he was only 11 years old and ruled for 60 years, during which the territory of Denmark was the largest in its history, but still, Christian IV had an eye for great architecture. He commissioned the building of the Royal Exchange (Børsen), the Round Tower, Trinitatis Church and Rosenborg Palace, Frederiksborg Palace, the spire to the main tower of Copenhagen Castle, the Blue Tower, and the restoration of the Kronborg Castle.

9. C. After her father's death, Leonora Christina was held prisoner in the Blue Tower of Copenhagen Castle – the very tower built by Christian IV.

10. D. Medieval knight tournaments were extremely dangerous, similar to extreme sports today, where people often get hurt. Even

the experienced knights could get injured, but they took the risk because, if they won, they gained fame and money.

Did You Know?

The knight's tournament typically lasted 40 minutes. In the end, the winner was proclaimed the best knight. The number of participants varied, but the largest tournament ever recorded in Denmark was held by Erik Menved in Rostock in 1311. It had almost 1000 participants, among which 948 were knights, 3 archbishops, and even 19 princes!

Identify the Pictures

1. When King Valdemar the Great and Queen Sophie married in 1157, the Danes made this event special by printing a series of small brackets with the image of the happy couple. It was the first time the king and queen were pictured together in Demark. According to the records, this is one of four methods used on the brackets.

2. The Danish axe became popular in Denmark during the Middle Ages (historians date its origins to around 1000 C.E.). It was used both as a weapon and for the construction of wooden objects.

3. The picture shows the reenactment of the Medieval tournament. As you can see, the participants wore colorful clothes and a form of armor. To easily see which knights were which, the knight's shields, coats of arms, horses' harnesses, and helmets were decorated with their coats of arms.

4. Like it's done today, minting coins in their name was a popular way to honor kings in Medieval times. These coins were created for Valdemar II, King of Denmark, 1202-1241.

5. It's a bronze belt buckle from 11th-century Denmark. It shows the intricate art often used at the time on clothes, accessories, and crafts.

6. The picture shows Hamlet costumes, displayed at the "Hamlet" or Kronborg Castle. The castle was turned into a museum, where you can see this and many other items related to its history and fame.

7. At first glance, you see the carving of a happy scene. People having dinner while musicians play their instruments around them. The carving is found on the front of a medieval chest displayed in the Frederiksborg Castle. Objects like this show how much the Danish nobles enjoyed art and used it to show their status.

8. The picture shows the ruins of the Hammershus fortress. Built in the 13th century, Hammershus was once the largest fortification in Scandinavia. It has a base castle residence, a grand tower, and a very long perimeter wall around the castle.

9. It's a medieval clock. As you can see, clocks in the Middle Ages were large and used in all homes. Still, they look impressive and complicated, just like many other art/craft items or even scientific tools from this period.

10. Princess Richeza of Denmark was married to King Eric X of Sweden. The Swedish king wanted to build a peaceful relationship with Sweden, which is why he married Richeza, the sister of the Danish king, Valdemar II.

Did You Know?

Kronborg Castle is located in Elsinore, which is why it's known as Elsinore Castle in Hamlet. Many also call it Hamlet's Castle. Strangely, no one knows whether Shakespeare ever visited the place. He had friends – actors whom he worked with – who talked about the beauties of Kronborg, but is it possible that Shakespeare was able to imagine and describe it just from their memories?

True or False

1. False. Denmark's medieval period lasted from around 1000, when it first became a Christian kingdom, until 1536.

2. True. Medieval Danish society was strictly divided into social classes, especially during the late Middle Ages (in the 15th and 16th centuries).

3. False. After Christian V fortified the Kronborg Castle in 1690, it was never used by the royal family again. From 1785 to 1923, it was used by the military and restored to its former state as built by Frederik II and Christian IV.

4. False. The dukes of Schleswig didn't have a good relationship with the Danish monarchs. Erik V even built a castle to defend against the dukes' attacks.

5. The castles of Koldinghus and Riberhus were saved from demolition because they were important defense points in the kingdom's southern border.

6. True. Shortly after 1320, Koldingus was taken over by the counts of Holstein. They occupied it until Valdemar Atterdag returned it

under Danish rule in 1348.

7. True. Now known as the patron saint of Denmark, Canute IV was not only the first Danish ruler but also the first Dane to be canonized.

8. False. Demark's reign as the maritime empire of the Northern Seas lasted only until 1332, when Christoffer II was forced to surrender some of the Danish provinces to the counts of Holstein.

9. True. Between 1242 and 1320, Denmark switched to a commercial economy, which led to the country's urbanization and economic growth.

10. True. While the alliance with Norway cost Denmark its independence, it also granted security if the Germans decided to attack and conquer the Danish territories.

Did You Know?

In 1320, the Danish nobility was so powerful that it forced the king (Christoffer II) to sign a charter before he was crowned. The charter claimed that all royal castles in Jutland must be destroyed, another way to diminish the king's power.

Match the Danish Medieval Celebrities to their Actions

1. Holger Danske (Ogier the Dane) – Conquered all the countries from Jerusalem at the center of the world.

2. Margrethe of Denmark – One of the few female regents who ruled over several countries in the Middle Ages (Denmark, Norway, and Sweden).

3. Canute – Martyred king of Denmark, sometimes called Knud.

4. Saxo Grammaticus – Historian who first wrote about Hamlet.

5. Valdemar II – The king who made Denmark prosper through new laws and survived three years in Black Henry's prison.

6. Absalon – Bishop of Roskilde and later Archbishop of Lund.

7. Sir Henrik Svane – Noble knight and lord of Sundkøbing, who held numerous knight tournaments. Fought against many other brave knights not only from Denmark but also from Sweden and other countries.

8. Niels Ebbesen – The national hero whose actions marked the beginning of Denmark's liberation.

9. Esbern the Resolute – Crusader and chancellor to Valdemar the Great.

10. Erik Klipping – Built one of Denmark's few castles that survived the Medieval times.

Multiple Choice II

1. D. The Manor houses or manorial farms were country homes owned by Danish noblemen. They were part of the medieval feudal system from the early Middle Ages.

2. A. The status of a manor house or manorial home was only partially tied to the owner's status. Manor houses were used as homes by wealthy farmer families. The owner could change its purpose (they could stop living in it), but this meant the home or farm's status was lost, too. However, the owner would choose to use another one of his properties as a manor house/farm. In this case, the new property gained the manorial status.

3. B. During this period, Denmark was called the Valdemarian Kingdom as it was founded by King Valdemar I. This was the second period of the great maritime empire of Denmark, lasting from 1157 to 1332.

4. D. The Kalmar Union united the countries Norway, Sweden, and Denmark. It was founded due to the efforts of Queen Margaret and was led by her grand-nephew, Erik the Pomeranian.

5. A. The courtly customs in Medieval Denmark were mainly different from Norway's. Unlike the Norwegians, who translated French and English texts that helped them become more chivalrous and less like the crusader knights, the Danish only used the German language at the court, which had very few resources for proper court behavior.

6. A. Denmark had a much richer history of traditions. Due to all the traditions carried from different cultures, the Danish court was also different.

7. D. When Valdemar IV died, the electors named Margrethe's young son, Olaf II, the new king. As he was too young to rule, Margrethe ruled instead of him, continuing the work of her father, who regained many territories from the Germans and Swedes. Her husband, Haakon VI, the king of Norway, died in 1380, and their son died in 1387. As she and her husband already ruled Denmark

and Norway together, the Norwegians accepted Margrethe as a ruler. Still, she thought that a woman would be seen as a weak ruler, so she gave the reins to her great-nephew (although she continued to rule, even when the two kingdoms were joined by Sweden in the Kalmar union).

8. B. Erik IV and Abel were both sons of Valdemar IV. After their father's death, Erik IV became Denmark's king, while Abel became Duke of Schleswig. However, Abel wanted to take his brother's place and rule Denmark, too, not just a small Dutchy in Germany. It's believed that Abel killed Erik IV so he could call himself the king of Denmark 1, which he was only able to do for two years before he, too, died.

9. C. Denmark was an electoral kingdom, meaning that any king had to be formally elected by the people (known as the magnates) at the things of Viborg (Jutland), Lund (Scania), and Ringsted (Zealand).

10. A. The Hvide were a powerful magnate kin group and close allies of the kings. They supported and provided military power to the Danish kings against Sweden and the wars in the Baltic Rim.

Chapter 3

Multiple Choice Questions

1. A. Tycho Brahe is one of the most famous Danish astronomers ever. He is known for his groundbreaking observations of the heavens, including the discovery of new stars and comets. Johannes Kepler partially adopted his observations, which later formed the modern theory of the solar system.

2. B. In 1596, Tycho Brahe published Epistolarvm astronomicarvm libri, a summary of astronomical observations he made while working in his private observatory. The document also contained his theories about the structure of the Solar system.

3. C. At the end of the 16th century, Tycho Brahe was contacted by German mathematician and astrologer Johannes Kepler. Kepler was interested in learning how Brahe determined that the planets circled around the sun while the sun, moon, and stars moved around Earth. He also hoped that the details of Brahe's research would show him whether the Earth was the center of the universe, as Brahe claimed.

4. D. Once they started working together, Brahe suggested that Kepler study the unusual movement of Mars. According to Brahe and other astronomers at the time, Mars didn't move like any other planet (it sometimes appeared to be moving backward, as observed), which meant determining how the planets truly moved was even more complicated.

5. C. Frederik II was a great supporter of science. When he heard that one of the leading customers, Tycho Brahe, wanted to leave the country to work in another European court, the king offered him his own private island. On this island given to Brahe, the king also built him an observatory, complete with the best technology at the time.

6. A. After teaming up with Kepler, Tycho Brahe started consulting with Kepler's primary employer, Holy Roman Emperor Rudolf II. The emperor was just as much a supporter of science as the Danish king. When he heard Kepler took Brahe as an assistant, he readily offered his protection and support to the Danish astronomer.

7. B. Due to his support of art, science, and booming culture during the era, Christian IV became known as the father of the Danish Renaissance. While his father, Frederik II, laid the foundation stone of the country's Renaissance era, it was Christian IV who made Denmark shine in lavish prosperity. From cities to castles to other landmarks, his name is tied to everything from the Renaissance period.

8. C. When Frederik II came to the throne, Denmark was already a powerful kingdom. Wanting to make it even stronger, the king decided to invest in scientific research that would help him achieve this. His attempt was successful, as the research led to many inventions that found good uses in the military, farming, and even everyday life.

9. D. Christian IV was much more a fan of ancient Nordic history and traditions than medieval culture. He thought it essential to preserve the Danes' origins in buildings and cities based on older, Viking-like models. He also ordered the writing of two history books, with specific instructions on how to depict Denmark's traditions.

10. A. While both history books ordered by Christian IV show Denmark as a powerful country, one of them puts great effort into describing just how much better it is than Sweden. This was likely due to the age-old rivalry and centuries of wars between the two countries.

Did You Know?

Similarly to today, knowledge meant power during the Renaissance. By investing in science, expanding their knowledge, learning foreign languages and customs, etc., the Danish kings opened the door to new opportunities. They gained allies and showed that they could be powerful allies as well – thanks to the new technology they invented.

True or False

1. False. Renaissance is an Italian word meaning rebirth. It means that a culture that was popular before the Middle Ages was born again.

2. True. The Reformation, during which the Danish state church became Protestant, began in 1536 – the year when the Danish Renaissance also began.

3. True. The kings of the era were extremely protective of the church and the arts and sciences. For the same reason, art from the Catholic era was removed slowly and handled gently. Even though it represented the past, it still deserved care and respect.

4. True. Before the German and Latin languages were used in court and during religious ceremonies, the Danish took over. Many texts were translated into Danish, sometimes with a little bit of change, but this only fueled the artists' inspiration to create something new.

5. False. Not only did the period give the royal courts more freedom to express their power, influence, and financial grandness, but the courts also gained a lot of money. Namely, many lands previously owned by the church were now taken over, and many of them were highly valuable or held treasures.

6. False. Noblemen also liked the splendor of art and decor. They built themselves richly-furnished manor houses decorated with the latest artistic creations. They collected jewelry, cups made of precious metals, weapons, and more.

7. True. While the wealthiest lawyers spent their days surrounding themselves with everything classical and valuable, those at the

other end of the social scale were becoming poorer than ever. They were often sick and excluded for committing a crime or an offense and spent their days begging on the street.

8. False. As much as they tried to increase their power by investing in art and science and gaining influential connections, neither Frederik II nor his son was able to make Denmark more powerful than Sweden. Thus, Sweden remained the ultimate power in the Baltic region.

9. False. Frederik II began building Castle Kronborg at Elsinore in 1574. It was part of the king's efforts to strengthen the Danish kingdom and gain a greater tactical advantage in case of an enemy attack.

10. True. Most surviving landmarks, architectural masterpieces, and literary masterpieces come from the Renaissance period. Moreover, the influence is also felt in neighboring Norway, which was under Denmark's rule during the Renaissance.

Match the Answers

1. Christiern Pedersen – Humanist and writer who translated Martin Luther's publications and the New Testament.

2. Anders Sørensen Vedel – Historian who translated Saxo Grammaticus Gesta Danorum into Danish and published the first collection of Danish medieval ballads.

3. Peder Palladius – Author of the Visitation Book.

4. Hieronymus Justesen Ranch – Author of the play, The Miserly Rascal.

5. Anders Bording – Writer of Danish Baroque poetry and founder of the first Danish newspaper, Den danske Mercurius (in 1666).

6. Thomas Kingo – A true poetry master who wrote in every poetry genre that was popular during the Renaissance.

7. Anders Arrebo – Writer of Hexaëmeron and translator of the Psalms.

8. Ole Worm – Author of Monumenta Danica, a book on runic inscription. He was a scholar rather than an artist.

9. Arild Huitfeldt – One of the most famous historians of the Danish Renaissance.

10. Hans Tausen – A talented spokesperson and supporter of the Danish Lutheran Church.

Did You Know?

At the beginning of the 16th century, Danish poetry had soft themes like love and religion, although hymns were also popular. In the next century, more classical patterns were seen, including works about scholars who also became highly active writers. By the mid-17th century, you could frequently read sonnets, alexandrines, or hexameters.

True or False

1. True. Like Italy, the birthplace of the Renaissance, Denmark also saw a revival of interest in classical Greco-Roman literature and philosophy.

2. True. While other influences were also seen, most Renaissance artists in Denmark primarily focused on religious themes in their artwork. They drew inspiration from religious texts (especially writers) and previous artwork. Some also portrayed how religion and similar classical motifs affected their own lives.

3. True. In the beginning, the controversy over the reformation was still strong, so many artists created paced to either support or speak against the Roman Catholic Church.

4. False. Christiern Pedersen, a famous humanist during the Renaissance, was the first person to translate the entire Bible into Danish. He finished in 1550.

5. True. After the oppression of humanity during the Middle Ages, showing human experiences became extremely important – even if this was achieved through classical and often religious themes. Besides being church-mandated, human ideals were also frequent in Renaissance art, which made a rich and truly enjoyable mixture.

6. False. During the Renaissance, the focus was preserving history and art, not religious structures. Most of the artistic effort was placed on creating magnificent castles, royal palaces, villas, and manor houses.

7. True. While many buildings were built by Dutch architects (whose work was very well paid for by the Danish king), Jorgen Friborg was one of the few Danish architectural masters employed to build or rebuild structures like the Frederiksborg Castle.

8. True. Many painters and sculptors found inspiration in French Baroque art during the Renaissance. This style is believed to reflect the king's taste as most artists were employed by the regent and lived among the royal court staff.

9. True. Caspar Bartholin the Elder was a prominent figure in medicine, and his research of the nervous system significantly contributed to future advances in anatomical science. His older son, also a medical scientist, Thomas Bartholin, created figures for anatomical publications. His younger son, Rasmus Bartholin, a physician and mathematician, is known for discovering the double refraction of the ray of light.

10. True. In 1539, two positions were created for teaching philosophical sciences. One was for physics, which involved teaching Aristotle's observations of physics and ethics. The other position was for mathematics, which involved everything from theoretical and practical arithmetic to Euclid's geometry to astronomy and cosmography.

Identify the Pictures

1. This is the Heart Book from the 1550s Denmark (During Christian IIIs rule). Its shape and the love poems and songs it contains speak about the romantic influences in Medieval literature.

2. The statue shows Tycho Brahe's unusually flat nose, which was a result of a catastrophic injury. When he was 20, Brahe challenged another scientist to a duel. He lost the duel, along with a chunk of his nose.

3. This is the portrait of Frederik II, made by famous royal painter Hans Knieper in 1571. It shows the classic elegance of one of the two kings who had a lasting influence in Danish Renaissance history.

4. This painting, Grape-Picker, is the work of Bernhard Keil, who was heavily influenced by the French Baroque style in the late Renaissance.

5. The picture depicts the wounded Christian IV talking to the crew of a ship called Trinity. While the painting was created much later, it shows the enormous influence this Renaissance king had on Denmark's history. He was well-loved by the people and often

depicted as brave and heroic.

6. It is the Old Stock Exchange in Copenhagen, one of the buildings with Christian IV's name tied to it. Besides funding its construction, the king also added the C4 monogram to this and every other building he erected throughout Denmark.

7. The picture depicts Renaissance motifs in Danish architecture. Danish architects were influenced by Dutch Renaissance Builders, and most of the materials used for buildings were also imported from the Netherlands.

8. This is a sculpturally decorated base from 1561 for a Renaissance building column. The artist is Melchior Lorck, a German-turned-Danish painter and printmaker.

9. This is the title page of Arild Huitfeldt's book, A Short Historical Description of Events during the reign of Christian II. Huitfeldt is one of the Danish Renaissance's most influential writers/historians.

10. This is the portrait of Niels Kaas, the Danish chancellor who acted as the leader of the aristocracy and the young Christian IV tutor. Throughout seven years, he thought the young knew everything he needed to know about ruling and helping his father's dream of strengthening the kingdom come true.

Chapter 4

Multiple Choice Questions

1. D. After absolutism was introduced during his reign, Frederik III continued the lavish court customs established by his father, Christian IV. However, unlike his father, who gave the manorial lords lots of freedom, Frederik's rule was more absolute and centralized.

2. A. In 1683, Christian V strengthened the centralized rule through Danish Law. The new laws ensured that the still-fresh absolute monarchy remained secure for many years to come.

3. B. For hundreds of years, manorial lords were among the most powerful people in Denmark. At one point, their power was even greater than that of the kings, allowing them to force the regent into decisions that benefited them. The introduction of absolute monarchy ended this. The king was given back the power to make decisions over the kingdom, and the lords lost their influence.

4. C. Enlightened absolutism was the dominant political ideology of the Danish monarchy from the mid-18th century. This ideology was based on the Enlightenment thoughts that started many new revolutions across Europe. The Danish Enlightened ideology resulted in reforms that transformed society and brought many benefits to the people. Rural communities gained more help, and the poor were given assistance to get better education and healthcare.

5. B. By the mid-18th century, King Christian VIIs health was getting worse, and he had a doctor, Johann Friedrich Struensee, living at the royal court in Copenhagen. The king trusted the German physician so much that he allowed him to become part of the royal court. In 1771, Struensee was named Privy Cabinet minister and had enormous political power. He introduced several reforms, for which he was considered the de facto ruler of Denmark. His "rule" didn't last long because the following year, he was convicted for lese-majeste (a crime against the regent, similar to treason).

6. B. Denmark lost the Scanian lands to Sweden, and Christian V started a war in an attempt to recover them. The war resulted in several long battles, known as the Scanian wars, which occurred from 1675 to 1679. Unfortunately, Sweden had allies in other European countries, so Denmark was unsuccessful in gaining back the lands.

7. D. During the absolute monarchy, the centralized administration system was divided into four parts. The Danish chancellery and the German chancellery were responsible for the legal system in Denmark and the German Schleswig-Holstein region, respectively. The war chancellery governed the navy and the army, while the treasure chancellery was responsible for financial matters.

8. A. Christian V introduced the Danish Code in 1683. It was Denmark's first legal code that allowed the county's administrator to work based on the law and not other influences. The Danish Code replaced earlier provincial laws and later expanded new legislation during the Enlightenment era.

9. C. Absolutism introduced hereditary monarchy, which meant that the throne could only be inherited – unlike previously when new rulers were elected by the nobility. Traditionally, this meant that the king's oldest son would inherit his father's place. If the king

didn't have sons, the throne would go to his younger brother, uncle, cousins from the father's side, etc.

10. D. Christian V's law of precedence determined social hierarchy based on royal service instead of birth, which meant the nobles had even less power in the royal courts. Many also lost status and could no longer attend important meetings.

Did You Know?

Christian V wasn't an experienced monarch. Unlike other kings, he wasn't prepared to rule, so he needed the help of his advisors to make important decisions. One of his main advisors was Peder Schumacher Griffenfeld, a powerful lord and the royal court's favorite. Interestingly enough, this wasn't the only time the current regent had advisors ruling instead of them.

True or False Questions

1. True. Absolute monarchs had unlimited power and were obligated to answer to anyone. However, they still relied on advisors and chancellors. Later on, they also listened to public opinion a lot when making decisions that affected the state of the monarchy.

2. False. Absolutism saved the country from political and financial losses when it was instructed in 1660. The Danish court slowly became more influential than ever, but this only lasted until the beginning of the 19th century. In 1814, Denmark was defeated during the Napoleonic Wars, lost Norway to Sweden, and lost all its political and financial power.

3. True. While the absolute monarchy existed until 1848, Denmark was already a poor and small country (when compared to its previous size, which included Norway and other territories).

4. False. While some Danish people moved to larger towns and the capital during the absolute monarchy, the majority continued living in the countryside.

5. True. Absolutism made the hierarchies in the society of estates clearer. Besides the small group of nobles that retained their status, there were layers of middling groups (farmers who bought their lands instead of inheriting them), merchants, master craftsmen, etc.

6. True. The different kings brought different styles to the court society. For example, Christian VI, who was a devout Pietist,

banned masquerade balls and evening parties. By contrast, Frederik IV and Christian VII held many balls and even had a theater troupe of twelve actors, allowing the people of the court to have fun and enjoy art. Unlike the previous rulers, who rarely showed themselves outside the castle, Frederik VI walked around with his family in Frederiksberg Garden every Sunday.

7. True. At first, absolutism was based on religious ideals and traditions, but this later changed under the influence of the Enlightenment. People could read about important matters in newspapers and books and discuss them during clubs. The courts saw that people's opinions were crucial for a strong rule, and at the end of the 18th century, opinion-guided absolutism was popular.

8. False. The absolutist monarchs no longer relied on noble advisors. Instead, they widened the role of civil servants, including them in administration processes. Many of these civil servants were highly educated, meaning they knew more about supporting the state's growing power. Some studied at universities in other countries, while others had a law degree from the University of Copenhagen.

9. True. Religion had a powerful influence on absolute monarchy, even during the Enlightenment. While the various rulers supported different religious ideas, these always played a role in their decisions. During the Enlightenment, religion continued to be influential, which led to many conflicts with the supporters of enlightened thinking.

10. True. Absolute monarchy in Denmark ended with the adoption of the Danish Constitution in 1849. This was the first free constitution, which was not ruled by any major political or religious ideology.

Did You Know?

Between 1650 and 1750, Copenhagen's population almost doubled – but this wasn't because more nobles moved to be close to the royal court. The increase was due to the centralized administration system, which required more educated people to live and work in the capital.

Match the Answers

1. Christian VI - The most religiously influenced absolutist monarch.
2. Frederik V - The most scandalous ruler, known for liking to drink a little too much.

3. Lord Chamberlain A.G. Moltke – One of Frederik's closest advisors.

4. Frederik III – The first absolute monarch who tried to limit the civil servants' power.

5. Christian V – Adopted the "divide and rule" policy, which meant civil servants had no specific power.

6. Ove Høegh-Guldberg – Crown Prince Frederiks teacher and a temporary ruler.

7. Caroline Mathilde – Queen to Christian VII, had a close relationship with Johann F. Struensee.

8. Karl Peter Ulrich – A Gottorp duke who allowed the Danish king to take over Schleswig and Holstein.

9. Crown Prince Frederik VI – Joined forces with Napoleon, which led to a devastating attack from the British army.

10. Christian D.F. Reventlow – Estate owner and leader of the Financial Chamber who resolved the issue of unpaid labor (which was caused by Struensee).

Did You Know?

Christiansborg Palace was one of the largest homes of Danish monarchs in history. It housed 800 court members. Another 300 people lived in the Prince's Mansion, which was close to the palace in Copenhagen. The Prince's Mansion is now the National Museum of Denmark.

Multiple Choice Questions

1. C. Barons and counts had the duty to report local crimes to the manorial court, administer court procedures, and collect fines from those convicted of crimes. In return, they didn't have to pay taxes, but this was one of the few benefits they had.

2. B. In the beginning of absolutism, civil servants had a lot of power, which meant that the king's rule was only as strong as their influence over the civil servants was. Later on, this changed as the servants were no longer given unlimited influence over specific matters, and the labor was divided between them.

3. A. To reduce the influence of civil servants, Frederik III started to put his signature on all court letters and documents. This way, everyone knew who was in charge and held absolute power.

4. B. Christian V often named favorites among his court officials. This meant that the most experienced officials would always compete with each other to gain the king's favor. He ended this practice after noticing that one of his favorites, Peder Schumacher, held too much power while supporting Sweden without the Danish court's approval.

5. D. The de facto rule of Johann F. Struensee ended after he was accused and convicted of a crime against the king. The accusation was first made by Juliane Marie, Frederik V's widow and the mother of his son, Frederik, Hereditary Prince of Denmark.

6. B. The Danish kings have resided in Copenhagen Castle for centuries. However, this building's open medieval-styled structure did not represent the values of the absolute monarchy and had to be changed. Frederik IV rebuilt almost the entire castle, giving it a new, lavish look. Christian VI was still not satisfied with the castle, so he completely demolished it and built the enormous Christiansborg Palace in its place.

7. A. Copenhagen's Frederiksstaden district was built by Frederik V in 1748. It was this king's way of showing his absolute power. The district was surrounded by four palaces, two of which later became royal houses (after Christiansborg Palace burned down and was rebuilt, but the royal family never moved back to it).

8. D. Court members spent their time playing chess, cards, or dice. The lucky ones had dinner with the royal family, while on special dates, all high-ranking court members were invited to magnificent banquets. During these events, people were treated based on their rank, reflecting the hierarchy of society (except during masquerade balls, when everyone was treated equally).

9. C. Club culture in Copenhagen became popular in 1780. The clubs were either public, giving more people the opportunity to discuss important topics, or scholarly societies, where educated people talked about the newest scientific discoveries.

10. B. The Supreme Court of Denmark was founded in 1661. Before this, people had to bring issues they could resolve otherwise to the king's court of final appeal. While the king was still the highest power at the Supreme Court, he had judges to replace him when he couldn't attend a hearing or ruling.

Did You Know?

After Johann F. Struensee died in 1772, the throne went to Frederik, Hereditary Prince of Denmark, who was Frederik V's only surviving heir. The new king co-ruled with his mother, Juliane Marie, and teacher, Ove Høegh-Guldberg. However, after 1784, his power was taken away by another Frederik, the Crown Prince and son of Christian VII and Caroline Mathilde.

Identify the Picture

1. Besides putting his signature on letters and documents, Frederik III also made it known which civil servants he trusted by handing out letters of privileges with the Coat of Arms of Copenhagen, as pictured above.

2. It's a monogram of Christian V, who, like Christian IV, liked to put his "signature" on the buildings and art pieces he commissioned to create.

3. It is a medal commemorating Christian VI after the king decided to increase the size of the Royal Navy. The medals' reverse side shows the fleet's ships, which are seen from the stern, with the sea god Neptune inspecting them. It was handed out in Denmark and Norway.

4. The portrait was drawn by Christian VII in 1775. It shows Johann F. Struensee and his friend, Enevold Brandt – the two people previously convicted of conspiring against the king. After putting his trust in Struensee for a long time, the king had a hard time dealing with the betrayal, and this drawing might have been his way of coping.

5. The picture shows the large Supreme Court hall in 1754, during Frederik V's reign. It is the work of Jonas Haas, the famous engraver from the 18th century who worked on famous buildings like the Copenhagen Magistrate in Gammeltorv Square.

6. This is the portrait of Crown Prince Frederik (soon to be Frederik VI of Denmark) meeting the young Christian VIII. The child was Frederik's father's half-brother's son and his future successor on the throne.

7. The touch drawing depicts a classic mid-18th-century Manor house. It's named Jægerspris Castle, and it definitely looks like a magnificent castle. It belonged to the Danish monarchs, who used

it to escape from the public and later served as a refuge for women.

8. An extravagant chandelier hanging in the Audience Chamber of Christian V. Based on the king's wishes, the chamber was built with a high ceiling, which became popular and marked the absolutism era architecture.

9. Frederik III learned that he was now the king of an absolute monarchy.

10. This was Gyldenløve, the newest model of Danish naval vessels, used from 1674. It was meant for the king, which is clear by the decorative elements that reflect the luxury of absolutism.

Chapter 5

True or False

1. True. The Kingdom of Denmark-Norway remained neutral from 1803 to 1815 despite pressure from both sides.

2. True. While the Treaty of Kiel ended the conflicts between Denmark and Sweden, it cost Denmark the territory of Norway. By surrendering Norway to Sweden, Denmark ended the era of the joint kingdom, which lasted from 1380.

3. True. France and Russia put pressure on Denmark to join its fleet to Napoleons because this would've meant that the British commercial ships would no longer sail to Nording ports (limiting Great Britain's export capabilities).

4. True. Danish ships (both warships and commercial vessels) were always known to be the strongest in Europe. The British didn't want to face them in battle and would rather have them in their own fleet.

5. False. When Great Britain asked Denmark to sign a treaty and give up its warships to Great Britain, Denmark refused. While the Brits promised to give back the ships when the conflict with Napoleon was over, the Danes didn't believe them. Moreover, Napoleon was threatening to invade Denmark from the south, so they needed all the power they had to defend themselves.

6. True. Copenhagen is located on the island of Zealand. By surrounding it, the British forces were able to cut off the capital from the other islands and the mainlands, making it defenseless.

7. False. Only after the British bombarded Copenhagen, killing 200 civilians and destroying many buildings, did Denmark surrender its ports and warships to Great Britain.

8. True. Given its location (the Napoleonic wars were already in full swing in Germany), the German duchy of Schleswig-Holstein was the most likely place for Napoleon to attack. Denmark concentrated most of its defense forces in this area, unfortunately leaving Copenhagen easy to defeat.

9. False. Despite surrendering after the attack on Copenhagen, Denmark didn't stay on the British side. Ultimately, Denmark allied itself with France, as King Frederik VI saw Napoleon as a powerful ally.

10. False. Frederik VI was a much-loved king, and he remained popular even after his decision to join Napoleon led to a national disaster. Their French ally lost the war, but the Danish people didn't lose faith in their leader.

Did You Know?

Denmark had a long history of conflicts with Great Britain and Sweden. Frederik VI thought that gaining Napoleon's support would be helpful during future attacks from enemy countries.

Match the Answers

1. Edmund Bourke – The Danish negotiator who signed the peace treaty in Kiel.

2. Christian Bernstorff – The foreign minister who worked closely with the then Prince Regent Frederik VI until 1810.

3. Niels Rosenkrantz – The second foreign minister under Frederik VI's rule and the one who participated in the Napoleonic wars alongside his king.

4. Steen Andersen Bille – A naval officer and Privy Counselor who played a crucial role during Denmark's state of armed neutrality.

5. Hinrich Ernst Peymann – The commander of Danish forces during the Second Battle of Copenhagen in 1807. Also signed the capitulation at Hellerupgård.

6. Johan Olfert Fischer – The commander who defended Copengahen from the British forces in 1801.

7. Lorentz Fisker was a Danish naval officer who organized the Norwegian defenses against Sweden and then Britain.

8. Peter Willemoes – A Danish naval officer known for his heroic actions and sacrifice at the Battle of Zealand Point.

9. Carl Wilhelm Jessen – Danish-Norwegian naval commander who led several battles against the British navy on the waters of the Danish West Indies.

10. Prince Frederik of Hesse – Danish nobleman who was also the governor of Norway during the Napoleonic wars. Later became the governor of Schleswig and Holstein.

Multiple Choice Questions

1. C. Denmark resisted the British attacks at the First Battle of Copenhagen in 1801, but eventually, they suffered defeat. Still, their ability to resist taught Great Britain to see Denmark as a strong opponent.

2. C. Frederik VI sent Crown Prince Christian Frederik to Napoleon's aid through Norway.

3. D. After joining forces with Napoleon to block British trade through the Continental system, Denmark lost many of its supporters. The alliance with Russia was now in the past, and the conflicts between Denmark and Sweden became harder than ever. Ultimately, the biggest consequence was being on the losing side in the wars.

4. A and B. When he heard that Napoleon had reached the border of Holstein, the Danish Prince Regent reacted by calling back his army from the southern districts of Holstein, hoping he could avoid conflict with the French. Soon after, he also commissioned a new naval plan, which included using lighter gunboats (which were more suitable for supporting the army) and rigs instead of the traditional warships.

5. B. Frederik VI met Napoleon in 1807 and found his character and quick-thinking skills very admirable. The Danish king was always more concerned with military strategies than with leading the country, so it is not surprising that the French Emperor's personality impressed him.

6. D. Despite the possible dangers, Frederik VI considered breaking the alliance with Napoleon. His only condition was that he

guaranteed the territorial integrity of his state, meaning the twin kingdom would remain as it was and wouldn't lose any territory.

7. A and C. In 1807, the Prince Regent of Denmark and Napoleon signed the Treaty of Fontainebleau, which said that neither leader could start negotiating peace with their enemies without the other's approval. Denmark and Napoleon also agreed on mutual support, with Denmark joining the Continental system and France compensating for Denmark's losses during the war.

8. B. Great Britain used the Baltic (including the Danish) ports to trade its own exports and colonial produce for precious metals and grains. It used these to supply its allies against Napoleon and keep its naval storages fully stocked.

9. C. Supplying the French army with food, weapons, and everything else necessary in wartime cost Denmark a lot. Eventually, the Danes knew that they wouldn't be compensated for these expenses, so they focused on preserving their states' integrity instead.

10. D. In 1812, Frederik VI offered Napoleon a secret treaty in which he offered to add 1,000 cavalry soldiers, 9,000 foot soldiers, and 50 field guns to the French forces in Northern Germany.

Did You Know?

Frederik VI calculated that the Russians would attack Napoleon's forces between the Zuider Sea and the river Oder and that the additional Danish fleet would help the French beat back any uprisings and landings on the Baltic coast. All he asked in return was a commercial treaty, which Napoleon never honored – despite accepting the extra help against Russia.

True or False

1. True. Great Britain and France both wanted to put pressure on the other's economy, making great efforts to limit trade in the European ports. This affected Denmark-Norway's economy from the beginning of the wars as the country's trade was also affected.

2. False. Denmark was also motivated by territorial gains. The German duchy of Schleswig-Holstein had previously belonged to Denmark-Norway but was lost to Prussia in a previous war. Napoleon promised that if Denmark joined its forces, he would help return the duchy under Danish rule.

3. True. After Napoleon lost the war, Denmark was in a terrible financial state. Besides losing Norway, the kingdom was also devastated by losing soldiers, warships, and trading opportunities.

4. True. While it was still neutral, the twin kingdom was concerned about a potential attack from Sweden. From 1773, Denmark had a close alliance with Russia (which included support against Sweden). However, this alliance was the kingdom's main defense strategy, which was proven to be a mistake.

5. True. Even at the beginning of the Napoleonic wars, Denmark kept its most powerful defense line, the navy fleet near Copenhagen. They were anticipating an attack from Sweden, and their warships were superior to the Swedish ones, so they were confident in their victory in case of an attack.

6. True. If Denmark had sided with Great Britain instead of France, Napoleon would have invaded Holstein, Schleswig, and Jutland. Denmark's largest grain shipments were coming from these territories, and losing them would've meant that Denmark would not have maintained its good relationship with Norway. Grain trade played a huge role in the relationship between the two kingdoms, and Norway's population (unable to grow crops under their harsh climate) depended on the shipments.

7. True. Frederik VI agreed to seek mediation between Russia and France. Napoleon also agreed to the mediation led by Austria, but he only did it to gain time and power over Russia.

8. False. Despite Frederik VI's hopes, Napoleon did nothing to support Denmark against Sweden during the heavy conflict period of 1808-1809. As Russia was at war with Napoleon, it also cut its alliance with Denmark, making the Danes much more vulnerable to Swedish attacks.

9. False. Upon learning that Norway would be separated from Denmark after 434 years of union, the Norwegians wanted to fight for their independence and refused to join Sweden. Denmark wanted to help them but was pressured to stop its assistance. Already in a very bad financial and political position, Denmark had no other choice but to accept this.

10. False. Even after witnessing several battles in which the Russians defeated the French, Frederik VI still believed that Napoleon would win the wars – as did most of Europe.

Identify the Pictures

1. The First Battle of Copenhagen. On the left, you see the British ships sailing into position to attack the Danish ships on the right. The way the Danish ships were positioned in line was intentional. They were to defend Copengahen at all costs – and they did.

2. Denmark-Norway. This was the twin kingdom's last Royal of Arms, in use from 1699 to 1819. Even though Norway was separated from Denmark in 1814, the joint symbol was used until several years later as the Norwegians fought for independence.

3. The picture shows the outline of cannon batteries around the island of Zealand. Similar defense strategies were planned after Denmark's defeat by the British forces in 1807.

4. It's the Duchy of Holstein. Napoleon's arrival here was a crucial moment in Denmark's history.

5. Niels Rosenkrantz. Surprisingly, it was the king's right hand who predicted that Napoleon would lose the battle against Russia.

6. This is Diana, one of the light gun frigates built in Copenhagen. It sailed to the Danish West Indies in 1807, shortly before Britain declared war on Denmark. The crew learned that the two countries were at war from a British vessel and immediately sailed to Spanish waters. Unfortunately, when Spain turned against Denmark, too, it captured the ship.

7. The Battle of Friedland in 1807. The picture shows the French cavalry quickly charging toward the Russian forces.

8. Count von Bennigsen, the leader of the Russian army, not only fought vicious battles against Napoleon but also outsmarted him a couple of times.

9. Napoleon met with the Russian Emperor Alexander I to sign the Treaties of Tilsit after Napoleon's victory at the Battle of Friedland in 1807. By this time, Napoleon had established his control over Central Europe, Prussia, and Russia, but he still needed Denmark's help against Great Britain and Sweden.

10. The Battle of Mobekk was fought between the Swedish and Norwegian armies during the Dano-Swedish War of 1808–09.

Chapter 6

Multiple Choice Questions

1. D. At first, population growth was larger outside the urban areas. Many people moved to the cities and larger towns because they simply couldn't find work in the rural areas. The labor market was more diverse and allowed for education so people could find different types of work. If they worked hard, they could earn higher salaries than in the rural areas. The towns were a great opportunity for traders and craftsmen, too, because commerce was booming, and they could sell their products for higher prices.

2. C. The first multinational companies opened in Denmark after 1880, when agriculture became increasingly industrialized, and new industrial enterprises emerged in the towns and cities.

3. A. The change in the economy simply meant that people didn't make enough money from agriculture, and the country had to look for other ways to generate income. This is where the Industrial Revolution and the new technologies came to help as they provided work and wage-earning opportunities.

4. Denmark adopted a market-oriented economy, which meant that companies worked toward their own success based on what they could offer on the market.

5. A and B. Market-oriented commerce involves getting the products to the market that wants them. This was made possible by building many new railways, harbors, and roads. The new telecommunication technologies, like the telegraph and postal systems, also helped make this new market successful.

6. D. Denmark's fast-growing urban societies were divided into an upper and lower middle class and the working class.

7. A. Middle-class Danes found it important to earn and manage their own money and spend only what they could earn. They spent money on the most important things first, and if they had left over, they still spent it wisely.

8. C. Not surprisingly, middle-class Danes earned more money than the working class. In working-class societies, often both the husband and the wife had to work just to put food on the table. In the middle class, the wife often stayed home, and her only occupation was to be a housewife.

9. B. Unlike many other European countries, Denmark didn't have a well-built sanitation system in the 19th century. So many people moved to the cities, and the population grew so fast that there were serious hygiene issues in the urban areas.

10. D. Urbanization did not affect all craft businesses in the same way. Some, like construction, were growing fast because there was always a need for new buildings. By contrast, industries where the workforce was easily replaceable with new machines (tailors, basket weavers, shoemakers, etc.) disappeared.

Did You Know?

In 1847, Denmark's first railway, which was only 23 miles long, was laid down between Copenhagen and Roskilde. By 1870, almost 540 miles of railways connected the large cities and towns. Soon, private railways were also built, expanding Denmark's rail network to over 2,500 miles by 1910. After 1872, railway ferries helped the work of railways.

Match the Answers

1. Businessmen – social elite.
2. Service trade workers – Lower middle class.
3. Civil Servants – Upper middle class/Lower middle class.
4. Police – Public servants/Lower middle class.
5. Housewives – Upper middle class.
6. Bricklayers – Skilled (higher paid) workers.
7. Housemaids – Unskilled (low-paid) workers.
8. Teachers – Working class women.
9. Aristocratic landowners – Major landowners in urbanized towns.
10. Doctors – Upper middle class.

Did You Know?

The lower middle class included small business owners who also worked in factories or agriculture. If their business didn't succeed, they still had income from their work, but if it did, they could leave their position and rise to the higher middle class.

Identify the Pictures

1. A textile factory from Aarhus. As you can see, factories were much smaller than today. However, during the Industrial Revolution, Aarhus was one of the largest and most successful textile

manufacturers in Denmark.

2. This is a portrait of a woman working in the fields in Skagen in 1904. Located in the far north, Skagen was one of the towns that experienced the effects of the Industrial Revolution much later than the more central cities and large towns.

3. Working-class women in the cities and larger towns earned less than men, and gardening was one of these jobs. Women who weren't working were supposed to take care of every type of work around their homes, including garden work.

4. City growth. This expansion plan for Copenhagen was created in 1857, even before the Industrial Revolution hit in full swing. City officials knew that when people started moving to the city to work in the new factories, they'd need more space to live, so they planned for the expansion.

5. A locomotive part is shown in a railway journal. By the late 19th and early 20th centuries, the railroad construction industry was becoming so strong that people became interested in everything related to it, including locomotive parts.

6. Agriculture, or more precisely, dairy production. The milk arrived at the factories by train in large, sealed cans. The cans were put onto weighing machines and labeled according to their weight and the farmer who produced the milk. The cans were then opened and tested for safety before the milk was either transferred into bottles or made into other dairy products.

7. It was a private bank, and the banking industry was also developing quickly during the Industrial Revolution. In addition to depositing and giving out money, private banks also dealt with investment. The wealthier lawyers invested in companies and fast-growing industries, which earned them a lot of money.

8. Hans Jacob Møller was a bank manager, which means he belonged to the upper middle class.

9. The work of the famous Danish painter Peter Ilsted. The portrait shows the cleanliness and simple decor of middle-class homes.

10. Jens Christian Christensen was born into a low-class working/farming family. Through education and hard work, he became a successful politician and later the Council President of Denmark (a position equivalent to today's Prime Minister).

Did You Know?

As a result of urbanization, Denmark's population in the towns and cities started to grow much faster than it did in the rural areas. In 1814, only 20% of Denmark's population lived in urban areas, while the rest lived in the countryside. A century later, almost half of the population lived and worked in the cities and larger towns. In 1840, Copenhagen's population was around 120,000, while in 1911, it was 500,000 (almost 20% of Denmark's entire population!). Aarhus, the second largest city, had only 52,000 inhabitants in 1911, but this was also a growth from the 4,000 people it counted in 1840. By 1911, even the provincial towns had over 10,000 inhabitants.

Multiple Choice

1. B. In 1892, a spinning plant was established in Vejle on the east coast of Jutland, using ring spinning machines for the first time in Denmark. Another spinning plant was established in the same town a few years later, and together with some major cotton-weaving plants, this established the city's reputation as the Danish Manchester.

2. A. Statesmen Orla Lehmann was a passionate advocate for social reforms that would improve living and working conditions for industrial workers.

3. B. In addition to textile manufacturing, food processing and production were other significant industries that played a crucial role in Denmark's economic development during the Industrial Revolution.

4. C. Education played a role in all industries. Obligatory education for children was introduced in 1814, which allowed the new generations to grow up with a higher level of knowledge. Moreover, adult education was introduced in 1844, which kickstarted a movement where everyone started to have a better future in learning.

5. D. When constitutional monarchy was introduced in 1849, it brought several benefits. Shipping privileges that made water transport expensive were erased, making the transportation of goods and produce available to more people. Contractual freedom and freedom of association were established, and rights of ownership were guaranteed.

6. A. Farmers looked to use the new technologies to their advantage. They started founding cooperatives in 1882, which were more efficient ways of working. The large dairy and meat-packing cooperatives produced more than individual farmers. The buyers/traders focused on quality and fast results, and even the export benefited from it. For example, 30% of imported butter came from Denmark. By 1914, Denmark exported 60% of its agricultural products.

7. D. Lars Christian Nielsen invented a continuously operating centrifuge for skimming cream from milk in 1878 at the Maglekilde machine-tool factory in Roskilde.

8. B. From the 1890s onward, Copenhagen had the largest rise in conventional industrial production. Some of the thriving industries in the capital included textile, ironworks, and housing (the latter because the workers kept needing more space to live).

9. B. Denmark's industrial growth was mainly motivated by the demand from its own market. The new technologies introduced during the Industrial Revolution made more convenient products, and the Danes wanted more of them.

10. D. Finance, trade, and transport were fast-developing sectors after agricultural industrialization started. Products had to be transported to other places and could be traded for cheaper. This piqued the interest of the finance sector, which grew investment opportunities.

Did You Know?

Besides food production, large cities like Aalborg and Randers also employed workers in cement factories, paper manufacturing, railroad construction, and shipyards. Meanwhile, in Carlsberg, the now world-famous Carlsberg Brewery had scientists working on improving the beer brewing process. One of them, Emil Christian Hansen, discovered that many different yeast strains can give diverse brewing results. He also developed the process of yeast brewing, which allowed brewers to get the perfect yeast strain for a specific brew.

True or False

1. True. Steam-powered machines were faster and easier to operate. They were also cheaper to use, as they did not rely on fossil fuels.

2. True. In the second half of the 19th century, Denmark accepted several child labor laws that helped child workers in factories gain better working conditions. For example, they had shorter working hours, and they couldn't be given work that would harm their health.

3. False. Denmark refused to apply taxes even after the transport costs were so low that it became extremely cheap to import foreign grain. Instead, farmers started to export animal products like eggs, bacon, and butter. After all, they had enough grain to feed the animals and produce these items, so exporting them was an easy way to grow their profit without taxes.

4. False. The agricultural field had more workers than the technological industries until after World War II.

5. True. While it was slow to start, Denmark's industrialization sped up after 1870, allowing the country to grow more rapidly than any other in Europe.

6. True. The Duchy of Schleswig-Holstein was a major grain producer for Denmark. The loss of these territories (along with Norway) meant that Denmark now had to produce, process, and transport all the grains within its own limits.

7. False. More railways meant faster transport, which lowered the costs of all industries where the goods needed to be transported further away.

8. False. Industrialization and urbanization were major changes to the agriculture-led Denmark. Several times, the growth became slower or even stopped. Fortunately, what was lost during these periods was soon gained back when the next phase of growth began and was faster than the one before.

9. True. The industrialization of Denmark picked up speed as new technology evolved, and business owners were better able to raise capital at the bank.

10. False. Copenhagen was the first one to become an industrial urban society in the 19th century. The city had the most factories and settlements for factory workers.

Did You Know?

The wealthier layer of the middle class lived in large homes near the city's borders. Their houses had good-quality furniture and carpets on the floor. People liked to keep their homes clean and respect each other. Keeping these values was important to them because it separated them from those in the lower classes.

In contrast, the working class lived in one or two-bedroom apartments, where a family of up to six people shared one bathroom in the backyard. In Copenhagen, where most people were forced to live in a small space, it wasn't uncommon for people to live in tiny lofts or basement apartments either. The most unfortunate ones lived in so-called impoverished tenement houses, where so many people lived that they were barely able to do anything but sleep and go in and out of the home.

Chapter 7

Multiple Choice

1. A. Due to its position, Denmark controlled a large part of the Baltic waters. Both sides (the Central and the Entente Powers) suspected that the other would want to use Demark to block their entrance to the Baltic Sea. Wanting to avoid this, they started to pressure Denmark to join their side.

2. B. The Battle of Jutland was the largest naval battle of World War I. It threatened Danish centrality because it was fought in Denmark's waters. It was feared that being so close to the war, Denmark would be dragged into the middle of it.

3. C. The two warring sides heavily underestimated each other. Each one thought they could defeat the other quickly after a battle or two. Instead, the war became stretched out and was mostly fought on lands away from Denmark.

4. B. In 1917, Germany started a surprise submarine war, which came close to Denmark's watery territories.

5. A. Until World War I, 30% of the Danish animal products were exported to Germany and up to 60% to the United Kingdom. As this arrangement was beneficial for the warring countries – who needed to feed their armies – they agreed to maintain the usual export routines for the first couple of years. Germany was even happy to provide plenty of animal feed in return – just so they would get animal products from Denmark. However, when the Germans began their sudden submarine war, Danish ships began to get caught up in the crossfire, and the trade between Denmark and Britain became impossible.

6. B. The difficult trade with the warring countries led to a shortage of goods, especially in agriculture. Animal food became scarce, which meant that less food for people was produced. There wasn't enough coal for people to keep warm, cook, or use in factories to produce necessary goods.

7. D. Some people saw the opportunity to make a profit by selling cheap canned products (especially meat) of suspicious origins to those who couldn't afford to pay the much higher price for regular products. Named "goulash barons," many of these people took to the frontlines, where they took advantage of starving soldiers who didn't have access to any food resources at all and were more than happy to get any food.

8. D. During inflation, you can buy less with your money. The same happened to workers who had fixed incomes. They earned the same as before the war but could buy less – some couldn't even afford to rent anyone or buy necessities like food, clothes, coal, etc.

9. B. The state started helping people during the first year of the war when the Danish economy started to truly feel the effects.

10. C. The first decision of the Extraordinary Commission was to regulate the price of rye. Buyers (especially low-class workers from urban areas) were extremely happy with this. Small producers weren't too affected, so they were happy, too, but the large producers were not so much because it meant a larger loss for them.

Identify the Picture

1. A "goulash baron" talking to a starving man. These "barons" were easily recognizable because they were obviously well-fed, wore flashy clothes and a top hat, and often walked around with a lit cigar in their hands.

2. Part of the epidemic hospital, Øresundshospitalet. Hospitals like this played a crucial role during disease outbreaks as poverty increased by the end and after World War I. One of the major outbreaks was the Spanish Influenza, which was introduced to Denmark from France but came from U.S. soldiers sent to strengthen the Allied forces.

3. These seemingly wealthy gentlemen were the leaders of the Venstre before and during World War I.

4. An armband from the uniform of the members of Free Corps Denmark – the Danish volunteer soldiers sent them to fight on the eastern front alongside the German army.

5. The signing of the Molotov–Ribbentrop Pact, the peace treaty between Germany and the Soviet Union, made Danish leaders confident about entering into a similar non-aggression agreement with Germany, after which the Germans occupied Denmark.

6. Southern Jutland. Here, the Danish army "resisted" the German troops for a very short period before surrendering.

7. The structure in the middle of the picture is part of the Tunestillingen, the defense installation set up on Jutland to defend against the enemy during World War I.

8. HMS Furious, the British vessel that transported the fighter aircraft for the Tondern raid.

9. In honor of the church that served as a hospital for the Danish soldiers following the Battle of Braine in France.

10. The islands of St John, St Croix, and St Thomas are also known as the Danish West Indies. In 1917, Denmark sold the islands to the United States of America as they were another source of financial loss.

Fill in the Blanks

1. The dissatisfied workers tried to seek help by joining trade unions.

2. On 7 August 1914, the Danish parliament passed the August Laws, which allowed the interior minister to regulate food prices and trade with countries.

3. The Venstre was a peasant movement against the hereditary nobility.

4. Food rationing was introduced when shortages became greater in the last year of World War I.

5. According to Social Liberals, rationing should have been a starting point for a more equal distribution of wealth, while Venstre said it should have been erased after the war.

6. By the end of the war, the previously stronger farmers' organizations faced a powerful working class ready to defend their wages and fight for better living conditions.

7. To make the inflation less noticeable, the workers managed to get triple wages, but the employers often retaliated by providing unfair or unsafe working conditions.

8. During the last years of World War I, the Danish state tried to manage its finances by taking out large loans.

9. Even during World War I, neutrality was stretched out in the German direction.

10. The Tune Stronghold (a series of fortifications from Køge Bay to Roskilde Fjord guarded by 50,000 troops) was set up to protect the capital.

Did You Know?

Despite its neutrality, the Danish government agreed to help the Germans during World War I by laying naval mines in Danish waters against an incoming British fleet.

True or False

1. False. Danish workers had much longer work days before World War I, and their workdays got even longer during the war. Only after the war did the employers meet workers' demands to reduce the work hours.

2. False. The Danish state paid a lot of money for extra security forces that prevented people from being cheated out of their money. This put even more pressure on the already struggling economy.

3. False. Many people of working age were affected, too, which meant that when they became sick or died, their family lost their financial support. Moreover, the fewer people were working, the more the economy and the main industries suffered.

4. True. Production in many industries all but stopped, and the warehouses were almost empty. The state believed that by investing in production, they could strengthen the economy.

5. True. The investors bought the produce to sell at much higher prices after the war, but the prices they set were too high. People in the Baltic Region couldn't afford to buy these products, so the investors had to sell them at lower prices.

6. True. By 1920, Denmark was in debt; the Danish krone was losing its value, and it could only export very little. When the international recession hit, the German market collapsed, leading

to an even higher rate of poverty.

7. False. Even after the 8-hour workday was introduced, Danish workers had 48-hour workweeks because they regularly worked on Saturdays. They were also asked to work overtime, which was rarely paid.

8. False. After the outbreak of World War II, Denmark still wanted to remain neutral. However, seeing the Germans advance, it soon became clear that Denmark would not be able to resist for long.

9. True. The German occupation of Denmark lasted from April 9th, 1940, to May 5th, 1945.

10. True. When the Freedom Council began the resistance efforts in 1943, it led to conflicts with the German occupiers. As the number and intensity of the conflicts grew, it became a war within a war.

Did You Know?

In 1913, the unions working under the Danish Federation of Unions had 107,000 members. In 1919, this number rose to 255,000. This was no coincidence; unions provided a lot of support during and after the war.

Reflection Questions

1. Denmark chose to remain neutral during World War I because it wanted to stay independent. Danish leaders feared that if the country joined the war and ended up on the losing side, it would be occupied by the winner and lose its independence. Ultimately, this was the right decision because by staying neutral, Denmark also maintained its independence.

2. The Kanslergade Agreement of 1933 determined that the worker's wages would stay the same, but the Danish krone would be worth 10% less, which meant that the workers could buy more with their money. Property taxes for farmers were lowered. The farmers could also export and pay their workers the same as they did before, but the workers would be more satisfied and would be able to sustain their families. Moreover, the agreement contained new rules for managing debt and buying beef from the farmers. Workers also benefited by gaining new houses and other help in the public sector (education, healthcare, social aid, etc).

3. The Tondern raid was an attack on the German base at Tonder (now a town in Norway) in the Baltic region of Jutland. The British Royal Navy and Royal Air Force destroyed the base during the

raid.

4. The mining of Danish waters. In addition to using submarines against the British fleet, the Germans also laid underwater mines in Danish waters to surprise the incoming British ships. The problem was that they sometimes sunk Danish trade ships, too.

5. The now-Southern Jutland region included the Province of Schleswig-Holstein, which was under Prussian rule during World War I. However, as the area had previously belonged to Denmark, the majority of its population was Danish. This was how 30,000 Danish soldiers fought under German command during the war.

6. The Germans pressured the Danish Social Democrat leaders to support agriculture and industry instead of giving better wages to the workers. This was an attempt to control the labor movement, which was linked to Communist forces.

7. The German occupation meant that Denmark could no longer export to one of its main "customers," the United Kingdom. With nowhere to send all the animal products it made, Danish agriculture suffered – and so did many industries connected to it (transport, trade, etc.). Some of the companies were closed as they couldn't handle another blow after already suffering losses during World War I. While the Germans bought some of the agricultural products and even provided coal and other items in return, this wasn't enough. Much like during World War I, the Danes suffered food and housing shortages, social polarization (they were either very poor or very rich), inflation, poverty-related diseases, and more. When even the government didn't help anymore, the resistance movement took over by sabotaging German military bases and Danish companies that produced supplies for the Germans.

8. **Marius Fiil** was the Hvidsten Inn innkeeper and member of the Hvidsten group, one of the largest and most famous Danish resistance groups. He and his family helped the British Special Operations Executive sneak parachutes, weapons, and other supplies into the country and distribute them to the resistance groups. **Jørgen Kieler**, a doctor and member of the Holger Danske resistance group, helped hundreds of Jews escape the Nazis and reach Sweden in safety. **Børge Bak**, a scientist and professor at the

University of Copenhagen, became a volunteer firefighter – which was a cover for easily collecting secret documents from bombed German territories and buildings.

9. In the beginning, newspapers like the *Land of Folk* ("Land and People"), run by the former and now hiding members of the Danish Communist Party, were crucial for organizing the underground resistance movement. Along with other secret organizations, the newspapers helped plan and share acts of sabotage, send reports to the British, ask for weapons from the British, etc.

10. After Adolf Hitler's death in April 1945, the Soviet troops occupied Berlin, and by early May, the Nazi forces in the Baltic region had surrendered. Since the fate of the war was decided elsewhere, the Danes learned about their freedom when it was announced on the radio. The first thing they did was take off the black clothes from their windows (these were used as shades during the bombing raids), take them to the streets, and burn all of them.

Did You Know?

While they only burned black clothes on the day of their liberation, the Danes continued this celebration tradition by lighting candles on the same day. Even today, over eight decades later, every May 4th, they light a candle as a reminder of the five long years the country spent in darkness.

Chapter 8

Match the Figures

1. Mogens Ludolf Fog – Doctor and member of the Danish Freedom Council. Founded the Frit Danmark, the resistance newspaper.

2. Monica Wichfeld – Raised funds for printing the underground newspapers and stored explosives, firearms, and ammunition for the resistance members.

3. Ellen Christensen – Worked as a nurse at Bispebjerg Hospital, where she distributed underground newspapers. She also hid Danish Jews until they could be safely transported to Sweden.

4. Povl Falk-Jensen – Leader of Eigil, a subgroup of Holger Danske. Known for capturing German collaborators.

5. Knud Pedersen – Artist, resistance leader, and founder of the Churchill Club (he was 17 at the time).

6. Kim Malthe-Bruun – A Canadian-born Danish sailor, the show used his sailing skills to transport weapons to the resistance groups.

7. Ole Lippmann – Member and parachute commander of the Freedom Council. Known for sabotaging bridges, railways, factories, and German military bases in Denmark.

8. Jørgen Haagen Schmith – Known under the codename of Citronen. Participated in the bombing of the Forum Copenhagen.

9. Bent Faurschou Hviid – Often called Flammen (flaming), after his bright red hair, who, together with Citronen, made the most famous resistance duo in Denmark.

10. Lone Maslocha – Daughter of Knud Mogensen and journalist who contributed to several youth resistance journals in 1942 and 1943.

Identify the Pictures

1. This unusual vehicle was built by Danish railway workers. Its armored outside was perfect for offensive maneuvers during the resistance.

2. Eric Scavenius, Danish Prime Minister who supported the German occupation and worked to push down the resistance by arresting members, spreading fear, etc.

3. Resistance members often fought the Germans on the open street. Here, they are fighting against several German soldiers on the street in Odense.

4. The Civil Partisans (Borgerlige Partisaner), also known as BOPA.

5. The members of the Churchill Club – a small but highly active group that regularly participated in sabotage.

6. Frits Clausen, one of the few Danish Nazi leaders. Werner Best, a German Nazi leader, wanted to make Clausen the leader of the Danish government, but Clausen didn't have enough support and votes.

7. The Danish Communist Party, whose members were later arrested or killed. Only a few of them escaped and started the resistance movement.

8. The HIPO Corps, the Nazi police force that replaced the Danish civil police, whose members were deported into concentration

camps.

9. The picture shows the arrival of the Danish Brigade in Helsingør. The picture was taken in May 1945, a few days after Denmark's liberation.

10. A commemoration of Flight Lieutenant R.H. Thomas and Flying Officer G. J. Allin, the Danish resistance fighters who died when their aircraft crashed in Maarum, north of Copenhagen. A memorial stone was placed in their name on the site.

True or False

1. True. After learning that Hitler planned to deport the Danish Jews to concentration camps in October 1943, the underground resistance transported almost 8,000 Jews to Sweden in small boats across the Øresund.

2. False. The rescue of the Jews wasn't an organized process. No one was prepared for it, but people from the underground organization came together very fast and helped in the best way they could. Some hid people in their homes, hospitals, or wherever they could until it was safe for them to leave.

3. True. Resistance members who served as lookouts in the harbors ran back and forth between the waterfront and wherever they were supposed to report. When they saw an opportunity to move safely across the water, they went to report this, but if transport wasn't safe, they stayed in their place in the harbor.

4. True. By 1945, occupying forces started retaliating against the resistance movement. As the resistance groups became organized and supplied, the occupation attacked civilians instead in retaliation for sabotage.

5. True. By 1945, resistance groups like Holger Danske were fully prepared to regain control from the German troops. Ultimately, it was due to their efforts that the Germans surrendered so easily in May 1945.

6. True. People believed that Social Democrat leadership gave too much control to the Germans, which made the economic conditions in the country worsen. The urban workers were particularly dissatisfied and threatened with strikes and rebellion after the war if their wages and working conditions weren't improved.

7. True. The German administration demanded that the Danish authorities punish strikes with the death penalty and set night curfews. As the authorities refused, the Germans stopped the peaceful cooperation.

8. True. While the Danish navy tried to resist, the Germans still disarmed it along with the army, which didn't put up much resistance (at least the official army didn't).

9. False. When the Germans saw that they needed more control in Denmark, they dismissed the Danish police and set up the Hilfspolizei (HIPO Corps) instead. Most of them were Danish Nazis and Nazi sympathizers – as these officers were easier to control.

10. True. The Gestapo was brought to Denmark only because the resistance movement became so strong that the German civil leaders and military didn't know how to fight it anymore.

Fill in the Blanks

1. The Danish government had asked the Danish press to stop criticizing Germany and Nazism to maintain a good relationship with Germany.

2. In mid-April 1940, Danish army intelligence officers known as Princes were reporting to London allies.

3. When Germany offered Denmark a reciprocal non-aggression pact in 1939, most Danish political parties agreed to sign it.

4. The German invasion of Denmark in April 1940 was part of a strategy for conquering Norway.

5. Initially, the Germans agreed to let Denmark remain an independent neutral state.

6. As time went on, all remaining Danish political parties collaborated more and more with the Germans.

7. After their victories in Belgium, Holland, Luxembourg, and France in the summer of 1940, the Germans started to make changes in the Danish government and leadership.

8. The new government leader, Erik Scavenius, encouraged the Danes to work toward better times and collaboration with Germany.

9. At Germany's "advice," the Danish Communist Party was banned.

10. In 1941, Denmark joined the Anti-Comintern Pact, a famous anti-communist alliance.

Did You Know?

When the Social Democrats agreed to meet the Venstre's demand to provide more support to the farmers, they had to take away money from somewhere else. Their solution was to reduce the workers' wages by 20% and compensate only minimally for price increases in rent, food, etc. Not only that, but the workers who weren't happy about this decision weren't even permitted to protest. The Work and Conciliation Board, which mediated labor conflicts, didn't have members from workers' organizations, so the resolution was rarely in the workers' favor.

Reflection Questions

1. At first, Danish citizens resisted through non-violent actions like spying for the allies (mainly British), distributing weapons to organized resistance members, and stealing Nazi weapons and supplies. Later on, they began attacking the German soldiers or destroying their supplies, along with the Danish factories that helped them. Others helped Jews escape to Sweden or disrupted the Danish railway network, delaying the Germans' advancement toward France.

2. The Danish resistance used sabotage and covert operations to disrupt German activities in several ways. These included destroying ammunition and food supplies, raiding factories before the Germans could get to them, destroying parts of railways and bridges to prevent the Germans from moving their army toward other countries, etc.

3. Communication under German occupation was very difficult for the resistance members. The underground newspapers and communication routes helped them keep in touch, send important information (like when or where to attack or sabotage a German move), and set up meetings.

4. One of the major challenges came from Denmark's civil leader, Erik Scavenius, who, as a German supporter, asked the civilians not to help the resistance leaders. Later on, the resistance members also faced threats from the Nazi civil police, who regularly tracked them down and arrested them. Many resistance members overcame these challenges by staying alert and sticking

together. As a group, they were always able to defend themselves better and inform each other of danger.

5. Many of the resistance groups helped each other, but they also gained assistance from the Allied forces. The British gave them weapons and parachutes. Some even moved to other countries to become British informants (for example, Berlingske Tidende journalist Ebbe Munck moved to Stockholm, where he reported the Germans' movements in Denmark to the British).

6. The HIPOs, known for their brutal attacks on known and even suspected resistance members.

7. The German occupation strengthened the Danes's desire for a true democratic state. It also showed that when the Danish people joined their forces, they could become stronger and overcome everything. Moreover, some of the regulation processes set up to revive Denmark's economy after the occupation helped the country thrive far more than it did before even World War I.

8. Many Danes didn't have a choice but to collaborate with the Germans. Some of them felt that they were betraying their own country, while others (like the workers whose wages were reduced because of the sabotage) felt betrayed by others.

9. There were two main motivations for the resistance groups. One was preserving traditional Danish values and systems that the Germans wanted to change or cancel. The other motivators came from communist circles, which were encouraged and financially supported by the Germans' main enemy, the Soviet Union.

10. People weren't satisfied because there was a shortage of basic goods. Moreover, the distribution of goods and financial help wasn't equal among all people. Agriculture gained far more support, while many urban workers lost their jobs or had wages that weren't enough for decent living conditions.

Did You Know?

The Danish resistance groups had many informers working against them, including Hedvig Delbo, a Norwegian dressmaker and Gestapo agent. She sold information about members of the Holger Danske resistance group for 20,000 Danish kroner.

Chapter 9

True or False

1. False. Denmark continued to share borders with German territories (through Schleswig) and wanted to avoid conflict. Instead, Denmark gradually began to revive trade, military collaboration, and cultural exchange with its German neighbors.

2. True. Between 1945 and 1973, Denmark's population increased by 25%. As the economy improved, so did the living conditions. More children were born, and people lived longer.

3. True. Better public health meant that fewer people died of preventable and curable infections. Most of these were bacterial (like tuberculosis, for example) and were now treatable with Penicillin. Childhood vaccination was also introduced against whooping cough, tetanus, and diphtheria.

4. False. Even though many of the temporary foreign workers remained in Denmark, they helped fill in the gaps in sectors where the Danes had seen shortages. In other words, they helped revive industries the Danes wouldn't have been able to revive on their own.

5. True. In the 1950s, the newly formed Nordic Council allowed workers from the Nordic countries to work and live in other countries from the region. This was the first relief for the Danish labor shortages.

6. True. The German occupation forces remained in one part of Denmark - that is, until the Soviet forces didn't take over these territories. The remaining German army fled toward the island of Bornholm and wanted to surrender only to the British. However, after a short bombing of the region, the Soviets took over and occupied the island until April 5th, 1946.

7. True. As it navigated the rebuilding of its economy, Denmark had to be very careful about political diplomacy.

8. True. Even as of 1955, the Danes lived in small houses or apartments, many of which didn't even have a bathroom. However, by the 1970s, the houses had become bigger, and over 71% of them had a bathroom.

9. True. During the 1960s, coal stoves were slowly replaced with a central heating system.

10. True. The new, larger homes were good quality, affordable, and had modern appliances. Due to the thriving economy, more people were able to afford technology like refrigerators, vacuum cleaners, and washing machines – none of which were common in pre-war Danish homes.

Did You Know?

Denmark's continued collaboration with Germany became one of the greatest examples of peaceful conflict resolution. It benefited not only the German minorities in Denmark or the Danish minorities in Germany but also the entire country of Denmark. As you remember, Germany was one of Denmark's largest export markets – regaining this market was crucial for reviving the country's struggling economy.

Fill in the Blanks

1. In the 1960s, Denmark went through a decade of high economic growth, which helped establish the modern welfare state.

2. By the 1960s, the industrial sector became the largest contributor to the state income.

3. By 1972, only 10% of the active workforce worked in agriculture, but there were more people earning wages as urban or self-employed workers.

4. The opposition believed that the welfare state was a bad idea because it would encourage people to rely on benefits too much and not want to work.

5. The Danish welfare state was based on Nordic values, as most countries from this region started introducing the system around the same time.

6. The welfare system was financed from taxes and not insurance, as in other European countries.

7. The state pension as a universal benefit was introduced in 1965.

8. The established welfare policy led to the building of many new hospitals and care homes for the elderly and children.

9. In the early 1970s, the Economic Council created two plans to set a sustainable budget for welfare expenses.

10. Every Danish person's health care, social security, education, voting, and military service rights were tracked by the CPR system.

Multiple Choice Questions

1. B. The Central Person Register (CPR) was introduced in 1968. It allows the state to easily track people's contacts, rights, and obligations to the public sector.

2. A. The first sales tax, known as *oms*, was introduced in 1967. It only applied to wholesale and not to retail sales.

3. D. To create a sustainable budget, taxes had to be increased gradually. Denmark's overall tax burden rose from 23% post-war to 40.3% in 1973.

4. A. After the municipal reforms, the local government had only two tiers. The lower one was occupied by the 275 municipalities, while the other was taken by 14 counties across the country.

5. C. In addition to a better welfare system, the economy also required the state to find lands for the rapidly growing industrial sector. More space was needed for new factories in urban areas.

6. C. One of the major advantages of the modern welfare state was that it benefited people of all ages. Unlike previous social support systems, which only aimed to help working-age people, the new one offered benefits from birth to death.

7. A. The concept of deserving needy, which essentially meant that people had to deserve their benefits, was removed from the modern welfare policy. It was replaced by the concept of right-based need, which gave every right to welfare benefits.

8. B. Industrial agriculture quickly outgrew all the other sectors. Motorization meant that fewer people and animals needed to be employed in farmlands and goods production.

9. D. Exporting animal products has always been a significant source of income for the Danish state. Combined with the effort to restore good relationships with old and potential new market countries, restructuring agriculture was crucial for reviving the struggling post-war economy.

10. C. Thanks to the modern welfare state, people lived longer. While this was a benefit, it also became a challenge. For example, before, the majority of healthcare needs were related to infectious diseases. Now, new illnesses, like heart conditions, diabetes, and

cancer, were emerging. Not only did people live longer lives, but they could also afford more unhealthy food, which could lead to these health issues.

Identify the Pictures

1. This Copenhagen building was one of the social housing projects that offered help for young mothers. From pregnancy care to giving birth to contraception education, women had access to many different forms of social assistance.

2. This is the picture of Bodil Begtrup, a Danish women's rights activist who argued for the construction of more public buildings and special collective housing assistance for housewives.

3. The members of the Nordic Council, founded in 1952. It gave uniform passports to the citizens of all member countries and the right to travel and work in any Nordic country they wanted.

4. The map shows the political and economic alliances during the Cold War between 1947 and 1955. Denmark had to navigate this complex international relations structure to rebuild its economy.

5. The Warsaw Pact was founded in 1955 to counter the efforts of NATO (North Atlantic Treaty Organization). Denmark relied on NATO for support and rebuilding its trade connections, which meant expanding to the Eastern markets. The Warsaw Pact was an obstacle in the form of a military alliance that made it much harder to establish connections in the East.

6. This is Per Hækkerup, the Danish foreign minister who introduced Denmark's new foreign policy. It relied on political, historical, military, and geostrategic factors, which allowed Denmark to navigate its post-war relations with NATO, the United Nations (UN), Europe, and the Nordic countries while rebuilding the economy.

7. This was a Treaty of Rome, which encouraged economic alliances among its members. Economic integration was very important for Denmark's foreign and domestic policy, as it meant more connections for support and trade.

8. The Marshall Plan, or the European Recovery Program, as it was known in Europe, provided Denmark with significant financial aid to rebuild its post-war economy.

9. The picture was taken at the nursery of a brewery in Hellerup. Nurseries in factories allowed women to enter the workforce even if they had small children. It was on-site, so when their workday ended, the mothers just picked up their children and went home.

10. The Lygten train station from around 1961. Trains and trams became important methods of transportation for the ever-growing urban population of Danish cities.

Reflection Questions

1. After World War II, Denmark rebuilt its economy slowly and carefully. They began reviving trade and investing in production. The more they produced, the more they could export, and the more people were employed in all industries. Improving working conditions for urban workers also helped because it made them more motivated to produce good work.

2. One of the key social welfare initiatives was the state mortgage scheme, which allowed people to buy new homes with only a small loan. More people were given social housing and had healthier homes and larger living spaces.

3. Women gained equal rights during Denmark's post-war period. They had a legal right to a state pension and guardianship of their children, but they also had equal duties to pay taxes. From 1962, women were able to join the Home Guard and the military.

4. Unlike the pre-war economic policy, the modern welfare state was based on equality and better living conditions for everyone. For example, before this state was founded, the children, the elderly, the disabled, the unemployed, the ill, and the students all depended on their caregivers (children, spouses, etc.). The modern welfare benefits included child and income benefits, student grants, pensions, rehabilitation and unemployment benefits, and more. Moreover, now, these benefits are right-based, meaning people who have the right to them can get them without much difficulty.

5. In post-war Denmark, more people (especially women) were able to get an education, and many had higher education. The higher their education level became, the more opportunities Danes had, which meant they could use their knowledge and experience to build the economy. The number of unskilled workers fell as more people were able to learn at least some skills. The new educational

programs also helped students of poor social backgrounds get higher education.

6. After a period of rapid growth, Denmark's population growth slowed down. This was due to the new social welfare and economic policies, as well as medical advancements. For example, people in rural settings didn't need to have so many children to help around, but the ones they had were healthier. Public benefits and contraception education allowed people to have more choices over family planning.

7. With greater benefits, people no longer needed to rely on their families for support. Not only were they less dependent on others, but they could also easily move to other places to seek better education and job opportunities. While preserving traditions was important to them, young people now had the chance to explore different values and cultures and find what makes them happy instead of continuing to live "as it was always done" in their families.

8. With the introduction of new technologies like machinery and automated work processes in the agricultural industry, fewer people needed to be employed in farms and agricultural factories. As they were left without employment, farm workers and their families often needed welfare support until they were able to find other ways to earn an income.

9. The trade, transport, and service sectors grew quickly because the state invested more in healthcare and social care. It employed more doctors, nurses, social workers, teachers, youth workers, and healthcare assistants, many of whom were women who joined the workforce in the 1960s.

10. When the divide between rural and urban municipalities was taken down, socioeconomic conditions in the two areas began to equalize. Social care and education were now decided on the state level, which meant equal opportunities for people in both urban and rural areas. All municipalities had the duty to enforce the rights of children and young people, regardless of their location.

Did You Know?

Denmark's economic rebuilding strategy relied on establishing tighter collaboration with other Nordic countries. However, orienting itself toward the West was also crucial for Denmark as this meant better security opportunities in the context of the new blocks that were being formed across the world.

Chapter 10

True or False

1. True. Danes are very trusting people. In their culture, they find that trusting others helps them avoid conflicts and even lower crime rates.

2. False. Denmark has one of the highest volunteer rates in the world. Whether it's helping those in need in their community, gardening projects, collecting waste, or anything else, the Danes are always up for volunteer work.

3. True. If it's an event within the city, the Danes will likely arrive by bike. Their bikes have baskets and larger transportation attachments with wheels, which are convenient for carrying whatever and wherever they need to go - including small children.

4. True. Compared to many other European countries, Denmark has few resources, but it uses whatever it has in the most creative ways.

5. False. Denmark has a very high number of innovations compared to its population size.

6. True. Thanks to their excellent social welfare state, low crime rates, and a strong sense of community support, the Danes have every reason to be happy. Even the relatively high tax rate can't bring their mood down because they know that their tax money is spent for their better future.

7. True. Out of Denmark's 28 Michelin-star restaurants, at least half showcase New Nordic cuisine - part of the New Nordic Wave influence popularized not only in the Nordic countries but also in other parts of the world (e.g., Tokyo, Sydney, Tulum, etc.).

8. True. Not only is education completely free, but university students are often paid to study. No wonder there are so many creative thinkers in this country!

9. True. Danes work hard for their money but they also like to enjoy their free time. They have five weeks of paid vacation per year to do this, and it's not uncommon for businesses to shut down for an entire month while the owners are on vacation.

10. True. Partly because of the foreign labor force, partly due to the technological innovation that connected it to other parts of the world, Denmark's culture became richer after World War II.

Did You Know?

Denmark continues to mount contemporary technological achievements. Ever since the 1990s, Danish scientists and companies have developed global innovations. One of these was Bjarne Stroustrup's invention and development of the C++ programming language, which became the base of modern software development.

Identify the Picture

1. Those are windmills on the Horns Reef wind farm in Jutland. Denmark has quite windy weather along the coastline, and the offshore wind farm is one of the best ways to take advantage of it.

2. This Copenhagen building has a ski slope on its top and a climbing wall on its side. The building that functions as a waste-burning station was designed by one of Denmark's top contemporary architects, Bjarke Ingels.

3. This island is called Samsø and is famous for its potato farms. Since 2007, it has relied solely on renewable energy, and the inhabitants have ensured that none of it goes to waste by insulating their homes. They're also working on a project that would fuel even the ferry that connects the island to the Danish mainland.

4. This world-famous chair shape (The Swan) was designed by Arne Jacobsen. Jacobsen was known for her modernist furniture designs, which include the Egg and the Ant chair.

5. The magnificent building of the Sydney Opera House was designed by Jorn Utzon in 1973. In 2005, the structure became a World Heritage Site.

6. The sign on the IC3 train honors Freddy Nielsen, the former chief architect of the Danish State Railroads and one of the most innovative industrial designers of the 20th century.

7. The bridge has a wide pedestrian path and an even wider two-way bicycle path. These types of bicycle paths are common on Danish roads and bridges – that's how serious Danes are about biking.

8. This miniature tram-looking structure is a playground. Denmark has the most creative playgrounds, especially in the cities. That's because most Danes live in apartments, so playgrounds are where

children have fun. In some places, adults can have fun, too, because there are cafes and restaurants nearby where parents can sit while their child plays.

9. This is the work of painter, stone sculptor, and graphic artist Henry Heerup. Most of his work is made from scrap materials.

10. Knud Illeris is a renowned processor who, among other places, taught at Teachers College and Columbia University. He also published several books worldwide – all of them based on his research on lifelong learning. The Danes have always shown an enormous capacity for learning, including learning from the past, learning from the present, and learning for a better future.

Did You Know?

Denmark is the leader in fiber broadband infrastructure, and the world's tech giants are beginning to notice it. They're investing in Danish data centers because they believe in the reliability of Danish telecommunication systems and because many of these are fueled by sustainable energy sources.

Matching Trivia

1. Holger Møller Hansen – In 1951, he invented fiber-optic imaging, the technology that transfers images to the eye with optical fibers. It's used for endoscopes.

2. Peter L. Jensen – In 1915, he invented the speaker while experimenting with wireless telephone systems.

3. Lars and Jens Rasmussen – Invented Google Maps while working at Where 2 Technologies in the early 2000s.

4. Susanne Koefoed – The Danish student who designed and first used the International Symbol of Access (ISA) to signal a place reserved for people with disabilities in 1968.

5. John Kirkegaard – Designed the first drum motor used for industrial purposes in the 1950s.

6. Elise Sørensen – A nurse who designed the first ostomy system (stoma bag).

7. August Krogh – First manufactured insulin in 1922.

8. Holger Nielsen – Danish athlete who formed the rules and invented the modern sport of handball.

9. Mikael Colville-Andersen – Danish-Canadian designer who coined the term "Copenhagenization" to describe the Danish capital's unique biking lifestyle and urban infrastructure.

10. Janus Friis – Entrepreneur and co-founder of Skype.

Did You Know?

The Denmark Pavilion, often used at prominent events like Milan Design Week, New York Climate Week, or the Olympic Games, is designed by Copenhagen-based architects. Its 600 chairs are made from discarded wood, fishing nets, and even recycled beer kegs.

Fill in the Blanks

1. A good work-life balance, a positive work culture, and support for family life make Danish people more productive.

2. Danish chef Brian Mark Hansen won the Bocuse d'Or contest, which is known as the unofficial cooking world championship.

3. When the Danes say hygge, they mean taking time off to do something for fun.

4. To the Danes, sustainability means using renewable energy, waste recycling, green transportation, and water conservation.

5. Denmark's effort to invest in sustainable energy is particularly admirable because the country has required heating for more than half a year.

6. Denmark operates the world's first carbon-neutral ship.

7. Denmark's ecosystems are so clean that the Danes can drink water from the tap anywhere in the country.

8. Denmark is known for activism for universal human rights across the world.

9. Jussi Adler-Olsen is one of the world's most famous Nordic noir crime novelists.

10. Smilla's Sense of Snow was a movie based on the novel by Danish fiction writer Peter Høeg.

Did You Know?

Denmark is just as committed to recycling as it is to using clean energy. If you buy a product in a bottle or can suitable for recycling, you'll be charged a small deposit. To get this back, you have to return the can or bottle. As a result, most Danes will return these items – especially plastic bottles, for which Denmark's return rate is 96%.

Reflection Questions

1. Vestas was the first Danish company to invest in wind energy technology. It has been manufacturing, selling, installing, and servicing wind turbines since 1945. In 2013, Vestas became the largest wind turbine company in the world and a global leader in sustainable energy solutions.

2. Godtfred Kirk Christiansen and his coworkers at his company (Lego) developed the Lego brick. The toy wasn't unique in itself but had a specific way of putting together the bricks, creating endless possibilities for its use. It became popular because it encouraged creative play in children worldwide.

3. The bicycle. Many Danes use bicycles as their primary mode of transportation, and their cities make this easy for them. Everything is within walking distance, and if they have to travel slightly further, they can always use the well-developed public transport system. The Danes rarely drive their cars (only to travel outside the city), and even then, they prefer ridesharing services for their environmental friendliness.

4. Biomass production in agriculture is a massive source of bioenergy in Denmark. The country has an extremely productive agricultural industry, so it makes sense that ⅔of its renewable energy comes from the organic material produced in agriculture. Some Danish power plants have even started to switch to biomass, leaving behind traditional fossil fuels.

5. Geothermal heat is another energy source used in Danish district heating systems. Moreover, some households use solar power to supply their energy consumption.

6. It means energy efficiency. Danes know that one of the best ways to create a sustainable energy system (whichever system it is) is to stop wasting energy. From energy-efficient appliances and home fixtures to using energy smartly, there are many ways to lower energy consumption in Denmark.

7. Denmark-based Arla continues the age-old tradition of producing quality animal products. Despite the large-scale production, Arla continues to reduce its CO_2 emissions. The company also uses recycled packaging and provides education on how to use its products, which include everything from milk and yogurt to infant meals to whey protein for sports.

8. Founded in 1945 by Poul Due Jensen in a home cellar, Grundfos makes every type of water pump imaginable. It's the largest manufacturer in its category and one of the giants that truly cares about minimizing its environmental impact.

9. Odense, which also has an extensive educational system, is the proud home of 120 robotics companies. From machinery and engineering to robot and automation companies (not to mention research facilities working on even developing newer technologies), this city is ready for the future.

10. In the 1990s, Denmark's telecommunications market was liberalized, which meant more affordable cell phone prices. The Danes were happy to embrace this new technology (along with the World Wide Web, which was also created in the early '90s) because they discovered that due to the country's flat landscape, they had a signal almost everywhere.

Did You Know?

In 2020 alone, Denmark produced half of its energy from solar and wind power. The country plans to increase this number and slowly leave behind all other non-sustainable energy sources.

Conclusion

Thank you for finishing this trivia book, and congratulations on all the fun facts you've discovered! To recap what you've learned on this eventual journey, Denmark has gone a long way since the Viking times. From master shipbuilders and ocean navigators who discovered parts of the world before everyone else, the Danes became settlers. Here, they fall in love with the land – and their love still lasts.

The Danish Medieval times were perhaps just as eventful, especially when it came to art, court customs, or rivalry among the royals. The period was followed by the Renaissance, which can only be described as the era of progress. This was the time when the Danish kings (not for the first time in history) realized that to become greater, they had to show that they could be greater. Fortunately, they did this by funding the work of artists, scientists, and architects – all those who left a lasting legacy for the world to see and discover.

The period of absolute rule was meant to bring some order into the chaos. Instead, it brought controversy because no king could rule alone (for some, the task was so big that they preferred to leave it in someone else's hands).

Due to its position, Denmark knew that maintaining a neutral position when countries around it were at war would be the best thing to do. However, when it came to the Napoleonic Wars, this wasn't possible. Denmark was forced to choose a side, and it chose the wrong one. As a consequence, a period in which the country was reduced to a portion of its size began.

The size reduction meant the loss of valuable resources that the Danish economy heavily relied on. With these gone, it was time for Denmark to reinvent itself – and the Industrial Revolution came just in time for that. Agriculture couldn't function as it was, so they rebuilt it by modernizing it. Factories grew like mushrooms, and workers needed more space, so they built homes for them by expanding the urban areas.

Unfortunately, they eventually ran out of space, funding, and support, so the workers had to make do with what they had. What they had became even less when World War I broke out. Once again, Denmark vowed to remain neutral – and it did, mostly. However, as the main parties of the war were Denmark's largest export markets, people still experienced shortages.

The country had just begun to recover when the next world war came, and this was worse. This time, neutrality was out of the question because the Nazis were bent on occupying Denmark. They had access to the Baltic Region (and snatched it off under the nose of their enemies).

After five long years of German occupation, Denmark was finally free and ready to rebuild itself once again. The Danish state invested in the revival of the economy and welfare state. In a series of genial tactical moves, it transformed the country that was on the brink of ruin into a leader in the Nordic region.

Modern Denmark has pushed its ability to create unique and useful inventions, and the country has been doing this since the beginning of its history. Now, the rest of the world has the chance to catch up and see the treasures and lessons everyone can learn from. Thank you again for taking the time to complete this book and learn these lessons yourself.

If you enjoyed this book, a review on Amazon would be greatly appreciated because it would mean a lot to hear from you.

To leave a review:

1. Open your camera app.
2. Point your mobile device at the QR code.
3. The review page will appear in your web browser.

Thanks for your support!

Check out another book in the series

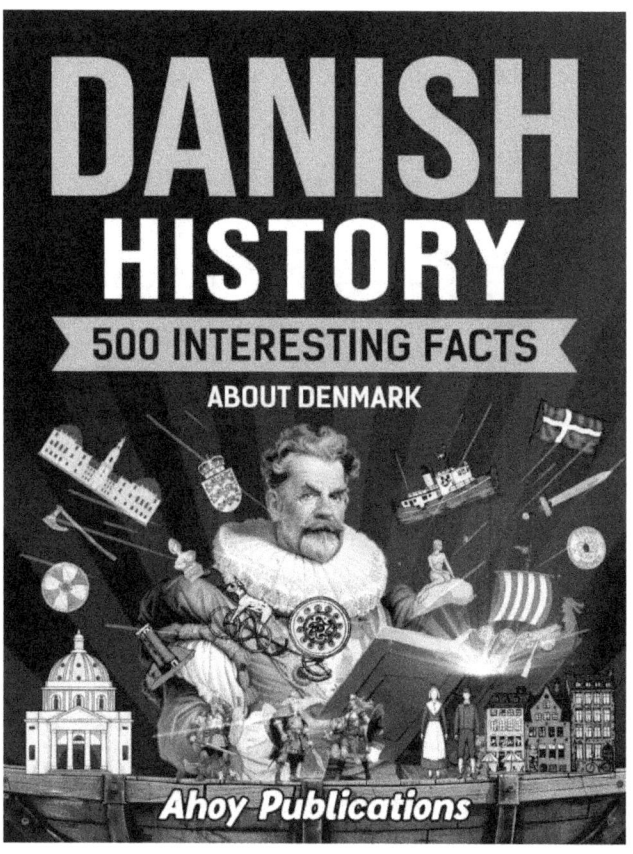

Welcome Aboard, Check Out This Limited-Time Free Bonus!

Ahoy, reader! Welcome to the Ahoy Publications family, and thanks for snagging a copy of this book! Since you've chosen to join us on this journey, we'd like to offer you something special.

Check out the link below for a FREE e-book filled with delightful facts about American History.

But that's not all - you'll also have access to our exclusive email list with even more free e-books and insider knowledge. Well, what are ye waiting for? Click the link below to join and set sail toward exciting adventures in American History.

Access your bonus here

https://ahoypublications.com/

Or, Scan the QR code!

References

538619@au.dk. (n.d.). 4. Cultural transformations and cultural struggles. Danmarkshistorien.dk. https://danmarkshistorien.dk/en/open-online-course/modules/module-9-global-times-after-1973/translate-to-english-4-kulturelle-transformationer-og-kulturkampe

538619@au.dk. (n.d.-a). 1. Denmark in the World War era. Danmarkshistorien.dk. https://danmarkshistorien.dk/en/open-online-course/modules/module-7-the-world-war-era-1914-1945/1-denmark-in-the-world-war-era

538619@au.dk. (n.d.-a). 1. The Danish realm and its population after 1945. Danmarkshistorien.dk. https://danmarkshistorien.dk/en/open-online-course/modules/module-8-the-post-war-era-1945-1973/1-the-danish-realm-and-its-population-after-1945

538619@au.dk. (n.d.-a). 2. The consolidation of the nation-state in the shadow of the world wars. Danmarkshistorien.dk. https://danmarkshistorien.dk/en/open-online-course/modules/module-7-the-world-war-era-1914-1945/2-the-consolidation-of-the-nation-state-in-the-shadow-of-the-world-wars

538619@au.dk. (n.d.-a). 2. The structure of society. Danmarkshistorien.dk. https://danmarkshistorien.dk/en/open-online-course/modules/module-5-absolute-monarchy-1660-1814/2-the-structure-of-society

538619@au.dk. (n.d.-b). 2. Denmark in the Nordic region, Europe, and the Western bloc. Danmarkshistorien.dk. https://danmarkshistorien.dk/en/open-online-course/modules/module-8-the-post-war-era-1945-1973/2-denmark-in-the-nordic-region-europe-and-the-western-bloc

538619@au.dk. (n.d.-b). 3. Absolute rule and the administration. Danmarkshistorien.dk.

https://danmarkshistorien.dk/en/open-online-course/modules/module-5-absolute-monarchy-1660-1814/3-absolute-rule-and-the-administration

538619@au.dk. (n.d.-b). 3. Ruptures within foreign and domestic politics. Danmarkshistorien.dk. https://danmarkshistorien.dk/en/open-online-course/modules/module-7-the-world-war-era-1914-1945/3-ruptures-within-foreign-and-domestic-politics

538619@au.dk. (n.d.-b). 6. The occupation, 1940-1945. Danmarkshistorien.dk. https://danmarkshistorien.dk/en/open-online-course/modules/module-7-the-world-war-era-1914-1945/6-the-occupation-1940-1945

538619@au.dk. (n.d.-c). 3. Economic growth and the welfare state. Danmarkshistorien.dk. https://danmarkshistorien.dk/en/open-online-course/modules/module-8-the-post-war-era-1945-1973/3-economic-growth-and-the-welfare-state

538619@au.dk. (n.d.-c). 4. Economic crisis and public regulation. Danmarkshistorien.dk. https://danmarkshistorien.dk/en/open-online-course/modules/module-7-the-world-war-era-1914-1945/4-economic-crisis-and-public-regulation

538619@au.dk. (n.d.-c). 4. Foreign policy. Danmarkshistorien.dk. https://danmarkshistorien.dk/en/open-online-course/modules/module-5-absolute-monarchy-1660-1814/4-foreign-policy

538619@au.dk. (n.d.-d). 4. Political culture – tradition and change. Danmarkshistorien.dk. https://danmarkshistorien.dk/en/open-online-course/modules/module-8-the-post-war-era-1945-1973/4-political-culture-tradition-and-change

538619@au.dk. (n.d.-d). 5. Economic development, colonies and agrarian reforms. Danmarkshistorien.dk. https://danmarkshistorien.dk/en/open-online-course/modules/module-5-absolute-monarchy-1660-1814/5-economic-development-colonies-and-agrarian-reforms

538619@au.dk. (n.d.-d). 6. The occupation, 1940-1945. Danmarkshistorien.dk. https://danmarkshistorien.dk/en/open-online-course/modules/module-7-the-world-war-era-1914-1945/6-the-occupation-1940-1945

538619@au.dk. (n.d.-e). 5. Cultural and social shifts. Danmarkshistorien.dk. https://danmarkshistorien.dk/en/open-online-course/modules/module-8-the-post-war-era-1945-1973/5-cultural-and-social-shifts

538619@au.dk. (n.d.-e). 6. Religion and the Enlightenment. Danmarkshistorien.dk. https://danmarkshistorien.dk/en/open-online-course/modules/module-5-absolute-monarchy-1660-1814/6-religion-and-the-enlightenment

Aarhus University. (n.d.). 4. Modernisation, internationalisation and urbanisation. Danmarkshistorien.dk.

https://danmarkshistorien.dk/en/open-online-course/modules/module-6-from-absolutist-composite-state-to-nation-state-1814-1914/4-modernisation-internationalisation-and-urbanisation

Christensen, L. (2010). DENMARK: THE TEXTILE INDUSTRY AND THE FORMATION OF MODERN INDUSTRIAL RELATIONS TEXTILE PRODUCTION FROM PRE-INDUSTRY TO THE PRESENT. https://natmus.dk/fileadmin/user_upload/Editor/natmus/danmarksnyeretid/Dokumenter/Industrikultur/Denmark_textile_history.pdf

Danish Patent and Trademark Office. (2021, April 21). Five Danish inventions with global impact. Www.dkpto.org. https://www.dkpto.org/news/2021/apr/five-danish-inventions-with-global-impact

Danish Royal Palace. (n.d.). Christian IV - Explore History - Kongelige Slotte. Kongeligeslotte.dk. https://kongeligeslotte.dk/en/explore-history/christian-IV.html

Dis Abroad. (2014, September 16). Top 10 Innovations Denmark is Proud of. DISCOVER STUDY ABROAD. https://discoverstudyabroad.org/top-10-innovations-denmark-is-proud-of/

European Route of Industrial Heritage. (n.d.). Denmark - ERIH. Www.erih.net. https://www.erih.net/how-it-started/industrial-history-of-european-countries/denmark

Feldbæk, O. (2001). Denmark in the Napoleonic Wars: A Foreign Policy Survey. Scandinavian Journal of History, 26(2), 89–101. https://doi.org/10.1080/034687501750211127

Frommers. (n.d.). Art & Architecture in Denmark | Frommer's. Www.frommers.com. https://www.frommers.com/destinations/denmark/in-depth/art--architecture

Henriksen, I. (2019). An Economic History of Denmark. Eh.net. https://eh.net/encyclopedia/an-economic-history-of-denmark/

Histories, M. (2012, March 7). Courtly Culture. Medieval Histories. https://www.medieval.eu/104/

History of Denmark. (2011). History of Denmark. Denmark.dk. https://denmark.dk/people-and-culture/history

Kristensen, N. B. (1989). Industrial growth in Denmark, 1872–1913 – in relation to the debate on an industrial break-through. Scandinavian Economic History Review, 37(1), 3–22. https://doi.org/10.1080/03585522.1989.10408129

Lindow, J. (2021). The Testimony of the Hoofprints. Ethnologia Europaea, 51(1). https://doi.org/10.16995/ee.1899

MacDonald, F. (2018). The Danish Network That Defied Hitler. Bbc.com. https://www.bbc.com/culture/article/20181001-the-danish-network-that-defied-hitler

March 2020, O. J.-L. S. C. 11. (2020, March 11). Lindisfarne: The "Holy Island" where Vikings spilled the "blood of saints." Livescience.com. https://www.livescience.com/lindisfarne.html

Middelaldercentret. (n.d.). Knights tournament | Middelaldercentret. Www.middelaldercentret.dk. https://www.middelaldercentret.dk/ridderturnering?lang=en

Ministry of Foreign Affairs of Denmark. (2019). Innovation and design in Denmark | Denmark's official website. Denmark.dk. https://denmark.dk/innovation-and-design

Ministry of Foreign Affairs of Denmark. (n.d.-a). Denmark is often cited as one of the world's best countries to live in. Denmark.dk. https://denmark.dk/people-and-culture

Ministry of Foreign Affairs of Denmark. (n.d.-b). Innovative solutions. Denmark.dk. https://denmark.dk/innovation-and-design/innovation

MrCaseyHistory. (n.d.). The Vikings: Raiders or Traders? https://mrcaseyhistory.com/wp-content/uploads/2019/02/vikings-raiders-or-traders.pdf

National Army Museum. (n.d.). Copenhagen Expedition | National Army Museum. Www.nam.ac.uk. https://www.nam.ac.uk/explore/copenhagen-expedition-1807

National Museum of Denmark. (2019). Renaissance (1536-1660). National Museum of Denmark. https://en.natmus.dk/historical-knowledge/denmark/renaissance-1536-1660/

National Museum of Denmark. (n.d.). Middle Ages (1000-1536). National Museum of Denmark. https://en.natmus.dk/historical-knowledge/denmark/middle-ages-1000-1536/

National Museum of Denmark. (n.d.). Modern Danish History. National Museum of Denmark. https://en.natmus.dk/organisation/management-secretariat-and-research-administration/modern-history-and-world-cultures/modern-danish-history/

Nobel Hviid, M. (2020, December 2). Christian IV and the use of history. Nordics.info. https://nordics.info/show/artikel/christian-iv-and-the-use-of-history

Nola Taylor Redd. (2017, September 13). Tycho Brahe Biography. Space.com; Space. https://www.space.com/19623-tycho-brahe-biography.html

Rasmussen, E. (1956). The history of industry in Denmark. Scandinavian Economic History Review, 4(1), 94–103. https://doi.org/10.1080/03585522.1956.10411485

Rosenborg Castle. (n.d.). Frederik II ♛ 1559-1588 - The Royal Danish Collection. Www.kongernes samling.dk. https://www.kongernessamling.dk/en/rosenborg/person/frederik-ii/

Rosenborg Castle. (n.d.). The History of Denmark 1800-1825 - The Royal Danish Collection. Www.kongernessamling.dk. https://www.kongernessamling.dk/en/rosenborg/1800-1825-2/

Rosenborg Castle. (n.d.-a). Christian V ♔ 1670-1699 - The Royal Danish Collection. Www.kongernessamling.dk. https://www.kongernessamling.dk/en/rosenborg/person/christian-v/

Rosenborg Castle. (n.d.-b). Johann Friedrich Struensee | The Royal Danish Collection. Www.kongernessamling.dk. https://www.kongernessamling.dk/en/rosenborg/person/johann-friedrich-struensee/

The Danish Research Centre for Manorial Studies. (n.d.). The History of the Danish Manors. Www.danskeherregaarde.dk. https://www.danskeherregaarde.dk/en/history/the-history-of-the-danish-manors

The National Museum of Modern Danish History. (n.d.). Modern Danish History. National Museum of Denmark. https://en.natmus.dk/organisation/management-secretariat-and-research-administration/modern-history-and-world-cultures/modern-danish-history/

The Nobel Prize. (n.d.). Physics in Denmark: the first four hundred years. NobelPrize.org. https://www.nobelprize.org/prizes/themes/physics-in-denmark-the-first-four-hundred-years/

The Royal Danish Collection. (n.d.). The history of Koldinghus | The Royal Danish Collection. Www.kongernessamling.dk. https://www.kongernessamling.dk/en/koldinghus/the-history-of-koldinghus/

Vaia Editorial Team. (n.d.-a). Viking Shipbuilding: Techniques & History. Vaia. https://www.vaia.com/en-us/explanations/history/viking-history/viking-shipbuilding/

Vaia Editorial Team. (n.d.-b). Viking Social Structure: Hierarchy, Roles. Vaia. https://www.vaia.com/en-us/explanations/history/viking-history/viking-social-structure/

VisitCopenhagen. (n.d.). Kronborg Castle | Hamlet's Castle, Elsinore. VisitCopenhagen. https://www.visitcopenhagen.com/copenhagen/planning/kronborg-castle-unesco-world-heritage-gdk1077722

Image References

[1] G.Lanting, CC BY-SA 4.0 <https://creativecommons.org/licenses/by-sa/4.0>, via Wikimedia Commons https://commons.wikimedia.org/wiki/File:Oseberg_ship_221.jpg

[2] http://creativecommons.org/licenses/by-sa/3.0/" title="Creative Commons Attribution-Share Alike 3.0">CC BY-SA 3.0:https://commons.wikimedia.org/w/index.php?curid=17219

[3] Toxophilus, CC BY-SA 4.0 <https://creativecommons.org/licenses/by-sa/4.0>, via Wikimedia Commons https://commons.wikimedia.org/wiki/File:Rekonstruktion_af_Ladbyskibet.JPG

[4] André Carrotflower, CC BY-SA 2.0 <https://creativecommons.org/licenses/by-sa/2.0>, via Wikimedia Commons https://commons.wikimedia.org/wiki/File:TV-009-0521_(15590080440).jpg

[5] Brianann MacAmhlaidh, CC BY-SA 4.0 <https://creativecommons.org/licenses/by-sa/4.0>, via Wikimedia Commons https://commons.wikimedia.org/wiki/File:Viking_Age_trade_routes_in_north-west_Europe.png

[6] Joe Mabel, CC BY-SA 4.0 <https://creativecommons.org/licenses/by-sa/4.0>, via Wikimedia Commons https://commons.wikimedia.org/wiki/File:Nordic_Museum_-_contents_of_a_Viking_grave_and_other_warfare-related_items_02.jpg

[7] Joe Mabel, CC BY-SA 4.0 <https://creativecommons.org/licenses/by-sa/4.0>, via Wikimedia Commons https://commons.wikimedia.org/wiki/File:Nordic_Museum_-_objects_of_adornment,_etc.,_case_1_-_01.jpg

[8] JC Merriman, CC BY 2.0 <https://creativecommons.org/licenses/by/2.0>, via Wikimedia Commons https://commons.wikimedia.org/wiki/File:Vikings_Glass_beakers_-_25807177032_Swedish_History_Museum_(Historiska_museet)_MuseumsPartner_exhibition_%22Vikings_Beyond_the_legend%22_Australian_National_Maritime_Museum_Sydney_2013.jpg

[9] Gilwellian, CC BY-SA 4.0 <https://creativecommons.org/licenses/by-sa/4.0>, via Wikimedia Commons https://commons.wikimedia.org/wiki/File:Valkyrie_fra_H%C3%A5rby.png

[10] https://commons.wikimedia.org/wiki/File:Germaanse_volksvergadering_(cropped).jpg

[11] Author of book and creator of the drawing of the bracteate: P. Hauberg (Peter Christian Hauberg) [1844-1928], CC BY-SA 4.0 <https://creativecommons.org/licenses/by-sa/4.0>, via Wikimedia Commons https://commons.wikimedia.org/wiki/File:Bracteate,_1157,_comemorating_wedding_of_king_Valdemar_(the_Great)_%26_queen_Sophia_(of_Minsk)_of_Denmark.jpg

[12] North Lincolnshire Museum, CC BY 2.0 <https://creativecommons.org/licenses/by/2.0>, via Wikimedia Commons https://commons.wikimedia.org/wiki/File:Medieval_Badge_(FindID_843534).jpg

[13] Maltesen, CC BY 2.0 <https://creativecommons.org/licenses/by/2.0>, via Wikimedia Commons https://commons.wikimedia.org/wiki/File:Copenhagen_Medieval_Market_(2482005861).jpg

[14] Hedning, CC BY-SA 3.0 <https://creativecommons.org/licenses/by-sa/3.0>, via Wikimedia Commons https://commons.wikimedia.org/wiki/File:Coin_minted_for_king_Valdemar_II_of_Denmark,_Valdemar_II_Sejr.jpg

[15] Christian Bickel, CC BY-SA 2.0 DE <https://creativecommons.org/licenses/by-sa/2.0/de/deed.en>, via Wikimedia Commons https://commons.wikimedia.org/wiki/File:Kbh_Mus_Bronzespange.jpg

[16] Yair Haklai, CC BY-SA 3.0 <https://creativecommons.org/licenses/by-sa/3.0>, via Wikimedia Commons https://commons.wikimedia.org/wiki/File:Hamlet-Kronborg_Castle-4.jpg

[17] Thomas Quine, CC BY 2.0 <https://creativecommons.org/licenses/by/2.0>, via Wikimedia Commons https://commons.wikimedia.org/wiki/File:Dinner_scene_carved_into_a_medieval_box_(Frederiksborg_Museum).jpg

[18] Helen Simonsson, CC BY-SA 4.0 <https://creativecommons.org/licenses/by-sa/4.0>, via Wikimedia Commons https://commons.wikimedia.org/wiki/File:Hammershus_ruin_Bornholm_Denmark_1.jpg

[19] Thomas Quine, CC BY 2.0 <https://creativecommons.org/licenses/by/2.0>, via Wikimedia Commons https://commons.wikimedia.org/wiki/File:Medieval_clock_mechanism.jpg

[20] https://commons.wikimedia.org/wiki/File:Richeza_of_Sweden_(1210)_effigy_(drawing_c_1860).jpg

[21] Fred Cherrygarden, CC BY-SA 4.0 <https://creativecommons.org/licenses/by-sa/4.0>, via Wikimedia Commons https://commons.wikimedia.org/wiki/File:The_Heart_Book.jpg

[22] Claus-Joachim Dickow, CC BY-SA 2.5 <https://creativecommons.org/licenses/by-sa/2.5>, via Wikimedia Commons https://commons.wikimedia.org/wiki/File:B%C3%BCste_Tycho_Brahe_in_Hamburg-Wandsbek.jpg

[23] https://commons.wikimedia.org/wiki/File:1581_Frederik_2._(cropped).jpg

[24] https://commons.wikimedia.org/wiki/File:Eberhart_Keilhau_-_The_Grape-Picker.jpg

[25] https://commons.wikimedia.org/wiki/File:Christian_IV_by_Vilhelm_Marstrand.png

[26] Alf van Beem, CC0, via Wikimedia Commons https://commons.wikimedia.org/wiki/File:Old_Stock_Exchange_Copenhagen,_pic-001.JPG

[27] https://commons.wikimedia.org/wiki/File:Gabriel_Engels,_Arkitekturmotiv,_,_KMSst589,_Statens_Museum_for_Kunst.jpg

[28] https://commons.wikimedia.org/wiki/File:Melchior_Lorck,_En_s%C3%B8jles_skulptursmykkede_fodstykke,_1561,_KKSgb5473,_Statens_Museum_for_Kunst.jpg

[29] https://commons.wikimedia.org/wiki/File:Arild_Huitfeldt_-_Christian_den_Andens_Historie_-_Titelblad_-_1596.png

[30] https://commons.wikimedia.org/wiki/File:Kaas_Niels.jpg

[31] https://commons.wikimedia.org/wiki/File:K%C3%B8benhavns_byv%C3%A5ben_1894.png

[32] Orf3us, CC BY 3.0 <https://creativecommons.org/licenses/by/3.0>, via Wikimedia Commons https://commons.wikimedia.org/wiki/File:Christian_Vs_monogram_(Bl%C3%A5_Karamel).jpg

[33] Nationalmuseet, CC BY-SA 4.0 <https://creativecommons.org/licenses/by-sa/4.0>, via Wikimedia Commons https://commons.wikimedia.org/wiki/File:Medalje_over_Christian_VI,_Orlogsfl%C3%A5den_1736.jpg

[34] https://commons.wikimedia.org/wiki/File:Christian_VII_-_Portraits_of_Struensee_and_Brandt.jpg

[35] https://commons.wikimedia.org/wiki/File:H%C3%B8jesteret_under_Frederik_V_by_Jonas_Haas_1754.jpg

[36] https://commons.wikimedia.org/wiki/File:Gerhard_Ludvig_Lahde,_Arveprins_Frederik_med_arveprinsen_Chr_VIII_,_1795,_KKSgb6510,_Statens_Museum_for_Kunst.jpg

[37] https://commons.wikimedia.org/wiki/File:J%C3%A6gerspris_Castle_1746.jpg

[38] Dennis Jarvis from Halifax, Canada, CC BY-SA 2.0 <https://creativecommons.org/licenses/by-sa/2.0>, via Wikimedia Commons https://commons.wikimedia.org/wiki/File:Denmark_0367_(4005211942).jpg

[39] https://commons.wikimedia.org/wiki/File:Nicolai_Abildgaard_-_Absolute_Monarchy_Assigned_to_Frederik_III_in_1660_-_KMS1139e_-_Statens_Museum_for_Kunst.jpg

[40] https://commons.wikimedia.org/wiki/File:Gyldenl%C3%B8ve_(ship,_1669).jpg

[41] https://commons.wikimedia.org/wiki/File:The_Battle_of_Copenhagen,_2_April_1801_RMG_BHC0526.tiff

[42] Sodacan, CC BY-SA 3.0 <https://creativecommons.org/licenses/by-sa/3.0>, via Wikimedia Commons https://commons.wikimedia.org/wiki/File:Royal_Arms_of_Norway_%26_Denmark_(1699-1819).svg

[43] https://commons.wikimedia.org/wiki/File:Map_of_the_batteries_atop_the_R%C3%B8sn%C3%A6s_peninsula_(Reefness)_in_1808.jpg

[44] Europe_1789.svg: *Blank_map_of_Europe.svg: maix¿?derivative work: Alphathonderivative work: Alphathon, CC BY-SA 3.0 <https://creativecommons.org/licenses/by-sa/3.0>, via Wikimedia Commons https://commons.wikimedia.org/wiki/File:Duchy_of_Holstein_1789.svg

[45] https://commons.wikimedia.org/wiki/File:Niels_Rosenkrantz_1757-1824.jpg

[46] https://commons.wikimedia.org/wiki/File:Thomsen_-_Fregatten_Diana_-_1809.png

[47] https://www.flickr.com/photos/fdctsevilla/4190063942

[48] https://commons.wikimedia.org/wiki/File:PPN663960002_Bennigsen_(1805).jpg

[49] https://commons.wikimedia.org/wiki/File:Tilsitz_1807.JPG

[50] https://commons.wikimedia.org/wiki/File:Battle_of_Mobekk.jpg

[51] Leif Jørgensen, CC BY-SA 4.0 <https://creativecommons.org/licenses/by-sa/4.0>, via Wikimedia Commons https://commons.wikimedia.org/wiki/File:Den_gamle_By_-_Tekstilfabrik.jpg

[52] https://commons.wikimedia.org/wiki/File:Michael_Ancher_-_Ung_Pige_-_1904.png

[53] https://commons.wikimedia.org/wiki/File:Julius_Exner_-_Fan%C3%B8pige_p%C3%A5_havearbejde_-_1898.png

[54] https://commons.wikimedia.org/wiki/File:Plan_for_the_Expansion_of_Copenhagen_1857_by_Conrad_Seidelin.jpg

[55] Internet Archive Book Images, No restrictions, via Wikimedia Commons https://commons.wikimedia.org/wiki/File:The_Street_railway_journal_(1899)_(14572958440).jpg

[56] Haggard, H. Rider (Henry Rider), 1856-1925, No restrictions, via Wikimedia Commons https://commons.wikimedia.org/wiki/File:Rural_Denmark_and_its_lessons_(1911)_(14781289891).jpg

[57] https://commons.wikimedia.org/wiki/File:Aarhuus_Privatbank_postcard.jpg

[58] https://commons.wikimedia.org/wiki/File:Hans_Jacob_M%C3%B8ller_by_G.P._Jacobsen_01.jpg

[59] https://commons.wikimedia.org/wiki/File:Interior_with_two_girls.jpg

[60] https://commons.wikimedia.org/wiki/File:Jens_Christian_Christensen_by_Peter_Elfelt.jpg

[61] https://commons.wikimedia.org/wiki/File:Gullaschbaron_tegnet_af_Storm_P._(DH014655).jpg

[62] Leif Jørgensen, CC BY-SA 4.0 <https://creativecommons.org/licenses/by-sa/4.0>, via Wikimedia Commons https://commons.wikimedia.org/wiki/File:Daghjemmet_%C3%98resund.jpg

[63] https://commons.wikimedia.org/wiki/File:Venstres_ledere.jpg

[64] From the collections of the Danish War Museum (Danish: Tøjhusmuseet); National Museum of Denmark (Nationalmuseet, Danmark); CC-BY-SA, CC BY-SA 4.0 <https://creativecommons.org/licenses/by-sa/4.0>, via Wikimedia Commons https://commons.wikimedia.org/wiki/File:WWII_Nazi_Germany_Waffen-SS_foreign_volunteers_Uniform_cuff_title_%C3%84rmelstreifen_%C3%A6rmeb%C3%A5nd_Frikorps_Danmark_Freikorps_Free_Corps_1941-1943_THM-27089_T%C3%B8jhusmuseet_National_Museum_of_Denmark_CC-BY-SA.jpg

[65] https://commons.wikimedia.org/wiki/File:MolotovRibbentropStalin.jpg

[66] Jutland_Peninsula_map.PNG: Rock Derivative work: Kolomaznik, CC BY-SA 2.5 <https://creativecommons.org/licenses/by-sa/2.5>, via Wikimedia Commons https://commons.wikimedia.org/wiki/File:Schleswig-Holstein_map.PNG

[67] Jørgen, CC BY-SA 3.0 <https://creativecommons.org/licenses/by-sa/3.0>, via Wikimedia Commons https://commons.wikimedia.org/wiki/File:Justitsraadshule.JPG

[68] https://commons.wikimedia.org/wiki/File:FuriousSP_89.jpg

---

[69] Alta Falisa, CC BY-SA 4.0 <https://creativecommons.org/licenses/by-sa/4.0>, via Wikimedia Commons. https://commons.wikimedia.org/wiki/File:18_June_1815_%E2%80%93_Victory_at_Waterloo_%E2%80%93_Braine-l%27Alleud.jpg

[70] I, Mali, CC BY-SA 3.0 <http://creativecommons.org/licenses/by-sa/3.0/>, via Wikimedia Commons https://commons.wikimedia.org/wiki/File:Dansk_Vestindia.png

[71] https://commons.wikimedia.org/wiki/File:DanishResistanceAC2795.jpg

[72] https://commons.wikimedia.org/wiki/File:Erik_Scavenius_1_(cropped).jpg

[73] https://commons.wikimedia.org/wiki/File:Members_of_the_resistance_movement_in_fight_with_German_soldiers_Flakhaven_in_Odense_5th_of_May_1945.jpg

[74] Julius Jääskeläinen, CC BY 2.0 <https://creativecommons.org/licenses/by/2.0>, via Wikimedia Commons https://commons.wikimedia.org/wiki/File:Armed_BOPA_members_with_their_Ford_Deluxe,_Copenhagen,_May_1945._(49513341566).jpg

[75] Churchill Club, CC BY-SA 4.0 <https://creativecommons.org/licenses/by-sa/4.0>, via Wikimedia Commons https://commons.wikimedia.org/wiki/File:ChurchillClub.jpg

[76] https://commons.wikimedia.org/wiki/File:Frits_Clausen.jpg

[77] Danmarks Kommunistiske Parti, CC0, via Wikimedia Commons https://commons.wikimedia.org/wiki/File:DKP_logo.svg

[78] Danish: Frihedsmuseet, Nationalmuseet Danmark: CC-BY-SAEnglish: Museum of Danish Resistance during World War II; National Museum of Denmark, Copenhagen, CC BY-SA 4.0 <https://creativecommons.org/licenses/by-sa/4.0>, via Wikimedia Commons https://commons.wikimedia.org/wiki/File:WWII_Danish_Hipo-Korpset_Hilfspolizei_HIPO_Corps_Efterretningstjeneste_ET_Nazi_occupation_collaboration_police_1944-1945_Uniform_collar_tab_FHM-317328_Nationalmuseet_Denmark_CC-BY-SA.jpg

[79] https://commons.wikimedia.org/wiki/File:Danish_Brigade_in_Helsing%C3%B8r,_May_1945.png

[80] https://commons.wikimedia.org/wiki/File:Denmark_After_Liberation,_1945_CL3181.jpg

[81] Source:seier+seier, CC BY 2.0 <https://creativecommons.org/licenses/by/2.0>, via Wikimedia Commons https://commons.wikimedia.org/wiki/File:Kay_fisker,_m%C3%B8drehj%C3%A6lpen,_copenhagen_1953-1955_(4037012544).jpg

[82] I Carried A Watermelon Dk, CC BY-SA 4.0 <https://creativecommons.org/licenses/by-sa/4.0>, via Wikimedia Commons https://commons.wikimedia.org/wiki/File:Bodil_Begtrup.jpg

[83] Nameyxe, CC BY-SA 3.0 <https://creativecommons.org/licenses/by-sa/3.0>, via Wikimedia Commons https://commons.wikimedia.org/wiki/File:Nordic_Council.png

[84] Goldsztajn, CC BY-SA 3.0 <https://creativecommons.org/licenses/by-sa/3.0>, via Wikimedia Commons https://commons.wikimedia.org/wiki/File:Cold-war-47-55-s.svg

[85] Fenn-O-maniC, CC BY-SA 3.0 <https://creativecommons.org/licenses/by-sa/3.0>, via Wikimedia Commons https://commons.wikimedia.org/wiki/File:Warsaw_Pact_Logo.svg

[86] Gobierno de Chile, CC BY 3.0 CL <https://creativecommons.org/licenses/by/3.0/cl/deed.en>, via Wikimedia Commons https://commons.wikimedia.org/wiki/File:Per_H%C3%A6kkerup.jpg

[87] Pona, CC0, via Wikimedia Commons
https://commons.wikimedia.org/wiki/File:%D0%A0%D0%B8%D0%BC%D1%81%D1%8C%D0%BA%D0%B8%D0%B9_%D0%B4%D0%BE%D0%B3%D0%BE%D0%B2%D1%96%D1%80.jpg

[88] https://commons.wikimedia.org/wiki/File:Marshall_Plan_poster_(cropped).JPG

[89] Willem van de Poll, CC0, via Wikimedia Commons
https://commons.wikimedia.org/wiki/File:Kinderverzorgster_staat_bij_een_vrouw_met_een_peuter_op_schoot,_Bestanddeelnr_252-9114.jpg

[90] https://commons.wikimedia.org/wiki/File:Lygten_Station_(early_1960s).jpg

[91] Hartmut Schmidt, Heidelberg, CC BY-SA 4.0 <https://creativecommons.org/licenses/by-sa/4.0>, via Wikimedia Commons
https://commons.wikimedia.org/wiki/File:Offshore_wind_farm_with_sand_bank_%22Horns_Rev%22,_Denmark.jpg

[92] Attribution 2.0 Generic CC BY 2.0 < https://creativecommons.org/licenses/by/2.0/>
https://www.flickr.com/photos/newsoresund/49141383237

[93] Jens Cederskjold, CC BY 3.0 <https://creativecommons.org/licenses/by/3.0>, via Wikimedia Commons https://commons.wikimedia.org/wiki/File:Udsigt_fra_Vesborg_Fyr_-_View_from_Vesborg_lighthouse_-_Sams%C3%B8_-_panoramio.jpg

[94] I, Sailko, CC BY-SA 3.0 <http://creativecommons.org/licenses/by-sa/3.0/>, via Wikimedia Commons https://commons.wikimedia.org/wiki/File:Ngv_design,_arne_jacobsen,_swan_chair,_1958.JPG

[95] Mfield, Matthew Field, http://www.photography.mattfield.com, CC BY-SA 3.0 <https://creativecommons.org/licenses/by-sa/3.0>, via Wikimedia Commons https://commons.wikimedia.org/wiki/File:Sydney_opera_house_side_view.jpg

[96] Kim Bach, CC BY-SA 4.0 <https://creativecommons.org/licenses/by-sa/4.0>, via Wikimedia Commons https://commons.wikimedia.org/wiki/File:Jens_Nielsen_(architect)_-_sign_in_danish_IC3_Train.jpg

[97] Kåre Thor Olsen, CC BY-SA 4.0 <https://creativecommons.org/licenses/by-sa/4.0>, via Wikimedia Commons https://commons.wikimedia.org/wiki/File:Odense-Byens_Bro-towards_north.jpg

[98] Leif Jørgensen, CC BY-SA 4.0 <https://creativecommons.org/licenses/by-sa/4.0>, via Wikimedia Commons https://commons.wikimedia.org/wiki/File:Playground_tram_at_Eilers_Eg_04.jpg

[99] Jens Cederskjold from København S, Danmark, CC BY-SA 2.0 <https://creativecommons.org/licenses/by-sa/2.0>, via Wikimedia Commons https://commons.wikimedia.org/wiki/File:Snowdrops_-_spring_is_on_its_way_-_Henry_Heerup_(1907-1993)_-_Granite_sculpture_-_Louisiana_Museum_of_Modern_Art_-_Zealand_-_Denmark_-_Flickr_-_Cederskjold_Photo.jpg

[100] Alex Spade, CC BY-SA 3.0 <https://creativecommons.org/licenses/by-sa/3.0>, via Wikimedia Commons https://commons.wikimedia.org/wiki/File:Knud_Illeris_(A).jpg

www.ingramcontent.com/pod-product-compliance
Lightning Source LLC
Chambersburg PA
CBHW061730120626
46550CB00005B/1757